OPEN PLAY

OPEN PLAY

The Case for Feminist Sport

Sheree Bekker and Stephen Mumford

Reaktion Books

Published by
REAKTION BOOKS LTD
Unit 32, Waterside
44–48 Wharf Road
London N1 7UX, UK
www.reaktionbooks.co.uk

First published 2025
Copyright © Sheree Bekker and Stephen Mumford 2025

Printed and bound in Great Britain by Bell & Bain, Glasgow

A catalogue record for this book is available from the British Library

ISBN 978 1 83639 053 4

CONTENTS

Preface

In September 2023, Tigst Assefa set a new world record in the Berlin Marathon of 2:11:53. As is usually the case, this is slower than the men's world record. One might feel resigned to the fact that men will always outperform women in sport. There is another way of looking at it, however. Browsing through the sporting records shows us that women can do anything that men can: it's just that, as things stand, they do it later.

Assefa's time would have been the men's world record until 1967. In sports where a direct comparison is possible, we see this pattern repeated. A women's high jump record of 2.09 metres was set in 1987, fifty years after men attained that height. In 50 metres freestyle swimming, the women's record in a long course pool is 23.61 seconds, which would have stood as the men's record until 1980. The most significant variable in comparing men's and women's sporting performance seems to be time.

Such facts challenge any claim that the difference in performance between men and women is either genetic or determined by some other immutable biological fact. There seems to be nothing that women are physically incapable of doing that men do, it's just that there is a time lag in them doing so. This time lag is not a vast one compared to the timescales of evolutionary change, so doesn't support a view that men are essentially or naturally better at sports than women. Instead, the data suggest that it is a difference in circumstances that is the key factor. Our aim in this book is to consider those circumstances.

Men outperform women in sport, in the sense of achieving sooner, because we live in a gendered world. We are assigned as either male or female at, or even before, birth and this has consequences for how we are treated over our lifetimes. A part of this is that our sporting arrangements are gendered too. Sport separates us into two distinct categories: boys/men and girls/women. Much progress continues to be made in sports science, of course, but these advances always, in the end, maintain a differential in treatment, opportunity, resources and rewards that ensure those in the men's category do better. In this book, we defend women's (and gender expansive people's) participation in sport while also diagnosing a major problem at the heart of *Women's Sport*. If women and gender expansive people were to have the chance to develop their physicality in the same way that boys and men have, we argue, then we will see that time lag reduce and possibly fade to nothing.

This book is a manifesto. We want to defend the idea that a woman participating in sport at all is still a radical act, highlighting the political significance of her participation. Yet, at the same time, we make a strong case against women's sport being a feminist win. We show that what, in this book, we call *Women's Sport* (the current arrangements for women in sport) is in fact a patriarchal tool. In this way, we then make the case for *Feminist Sport*.

Feminist Sport is not only about women. Our sporting activities have for some time been strictly divided by gender, as already noted above. It is a simple binary division, even though there are many people who cannot be so easily allotted to one or the other or choose to reject the division altogether. Need we arrange sport this way since it excludes so many people? We are defending sport not just for women but also for anyone who does not fit the binary, which includes groups of people with some of the lowest participation rates in sport.

More than that, we set forth a vision for the future of sport that is for everyone. We call this vision *Feminist Sport* since it challenges the established patriarchal order that hurts us all. Moving beyond patriarchy – a system of sex-based power – would bring liberation for everyone. Sport, it turns out, is one of the key platforms on which this more equal world can be built.

Sport, we maintain, is a feminist issue. It is one of the biggest. We have seen much feminist progress in other walks of life. In employment practices, in many parts of the world, it is no longer acceptable to assume that there are jobs specifically for women or men, or that men are intellectually superior to women. And we have been heading towards more equality in domestic arrangements, with fewer people thinking it 'natural' for household tasks to be gender specific. Nevertheless, sport remains an area in which all sorts of inequalities are considered natural and inevitable – where men are celebrated for their physicality while women's is suspicious. Women are permitted entry to sport and physicality begrudgingly and conditionally, and thought incapable of ever matching men. The (Western) world now seems to accept that a woman is the equal of a man, yet sport is the one domain that shows that there still remains a stubborn divide in what is expected of her. Our argument in this book is that the physical differences between men and women are constructed and manufactured rather than natural. We show that sport is currently playing a crucial role in shaping our idea of what it is to be a woman, physically inferior, and how the idea is then made concrete in the reality of women's bodies. Misogyny and patriarchy thus shape the physical being of women, in line with a view that French feminist Christine Delphy called Materialist Constructivist Feminism.[1]

Such a central role for sport, however, provides us with a great opportunity. If we can see women being celebrated for their physical being and achieving great things in sport, we can shatter the myth of feminine fragility to which our current arrangements contribute. Let us challenge those current arrangements, then, and see what women, and others, can do when liberated. It has rarely been tried and no one should presume to prejudge the outcomes. In particular, we think it wrong to make observations about women's 'inferior' performance under patriarchal control and presume that it would continue when liberated. The stakes are high here, as patriarchy recognizes and fears. If we were to show that women were also the physical equals of men, as well as their equals in all other respects, the whole established order could come crashing down. This is why those who truly promote women's interests in sport will be opposed, often violently, by those in power. Such a backlash we take as a sign of genuinely challenging patriarchy. Being gifted column inches in the right-wing press is not.

We are grateful to our editor Pascal Porcheron for originally suggesting this book. Like many others, he saw Sheree's Twitter (as it was) thread on women's ability to challenge men in sport, and the sporting authorities' reaction when they did (which forms the basis for Chapter Two). The thread had over 10 million views and, as is to be expected in the social media age, brought out many misogynist trolls. Again, this is a sign of doing something right. Sheree has a strong background in sport, in both competition and research. She swam at National level and swimming remains her perfect place. After degrees in human movement science and sport science, and her PhD on sports injury prevention, her research now has a social science eye, focused on gendered aspects, investigating how higher injury rates for women over men were made through cultural and environmental factors. Sheree was part of a team that looked specifically at gendered environments behind the high rates of anterior cruciate ligament injuries in women. This book represents a broadening of her work, considering more generally how women are made weaker in a world of sport created by men, for men and run by men.

Stephen is a philosopher who has worked in many areas. He has a background in the philosophy of sport but is currently disillusioned with the directions the sub-discipline is taking and rejects many of the currently prevalent views. He is aware of the pitfalls of being a man advocating for women and holding a feminist view. Nevertheless, he is persuaded that now is the time to speak up. Following Jenni Hermoso's unwanted on-screen touching by her football association's president Luis Rubiales, she and others questioned why it was only women who were protesting. Shouldn't men recognize and speak out against injustice too? Stephen wishes to do so here, as an ally. Why should it be an additional burden on women, who first suffer abuse from a system, to be the ones who have to then challenge that system? Another consideration, as mentioned above, is that patriarchy harms us all. Thus, even if you thought you should only write a book out of self-interest, Stephen is persuaded that he has sufficient interest in the advancement of feminism. As social activist bell hooks declares, feminism is for everybody.[2]

We both hold academic positions but do not want readers to see this as an (overly) academic book. We have avoided some of the trappings of academia, such as technical language and in-text citations. At the end, however, readers will find references and some suggestions for further reading. This was the kind of hybrid book we wanted to write: one that aimed to offer interesting, rigorous and compelling arguments but without excluding swathes of potential readers. We hope that all sorts of readers will be able to follow along. You certainly need no prior background in sports science, philosophy or intersectional feminist theory. The book aims to be self-contained, in that respect, and we just request of our readers an open mind and some degree of sympathy with gender equality as a worthy ambition. That should be enough.

We also wanted this book to be a call to action. We are well aware of how much we are asking. The changes we want to see in sport would amount to a revolution: one that requires the overthrow of patriarchal power. The role of sport in achieving this has been underestimated, we both believe.

In summary, what you will find in this book is as follows. In Chapter One, we set the scene by showing how important sport is to the perception of, and expectations put upon, women, their bodies and their physicality. We explain why we think the sporting differences between men and women are created rather than natural. Chapter Two makes the case for sport being a key feminist issue. We use a number of historical examples that explain the creation of *Women's Sport* as a separate category. The existence of this category is not a feminist win. Rather, its existence maintains the control and subordination of women, with the aim that women will never beat men again. Here, we take up the plea for feminist killjoys to stand their ground. Chapter Three contains a sorry catalogue of dubious sex testing in sport. Supposedly justified to preserve the integrity of *Women's Sport*, its effect is that all women must surrender their bodily autonomy as a precondition of sporting participation. Given women's systematic exclusion from the best that sport has to offer, wouldn't it be understandable if they rejected sport altogether and didn't participate at all? We address this possible response in Chapter Four but reject it. The physical development and flourishing that sport affords ought to be a human good for everyone. Patriarchy cannot preserve this field of human activity for men alone, even if that was originally the plan. In Chapter Five, we make the case against sport being sex-separated. This requires us to differentiate between (potentially good) protected spaces and (always bad) segregated spaces. Women's sport, we believe, is an instance of the latter. Sport should be sex-desegregated. But how can this be done? Should women's sport become more like men's? We argue not, in Chapter Six. Instead, we advocate for *Feminist Sport*: a new vision of sport for everyone but modelled on feminist values, and thus differentiated from both *Women's Sport* and (men's) *Sport*.

We finished the main text of this book in the spring of 2024, prior to the Paris Olympic Games. Other than this note, we are unable to comment on the progress, and eventual success, of Algerian boxer Imane Khelif. Nonetheless, we hope readers can see that our book predicts so much of her story. A non-White woman had her sex scrutinized and challenged for failing to meet the norms of White, Western femininity. She was not alone: Taiwanese boxer Lin Yu-ting was also questioned. Khelif, in particular, was under suspicion for being 'too strong' to be a 'real woman'. The attack on her was cruel and vitriolic: her lawyers described the abuse she received as an 'online lynching'. Her power in boxing was depicted as immoral and unfair, while a man's power in boxing never would be. Perhaps, most importantly, the incident showed that if we allow attacks on trans athletes to continue unchecked, and accept the patriarchal policing of women's bodies, this will quickly transfer to any woman whose body fails to match a certain narrow standard of femininity. Merely being good at one's sport will itself be an adequate ground for suspicion and abuse. This has been a further deterrent to woman's participation in sport: a deterrent that *Feminist Sport* aims to correct.

1

The Sports Bra

In the 110th minute of the Women's Euro 2022 football tournament final, England's Chloe Kelly whipped her shirt off in celebration of what turned out to be the winning Championship goal. Running towards her team's bench, she waved her shirt around her head before being surrounded by ecstatic teammates. In removing her shirt, the record Wembley crowd of 90,000, along with millions watching the broadcast live around the world, saw a woman athlete rejoice at her feat in her sports bra. By repeating Brandi Chastain's celebration with this same act in the 1999 World Cup final, Kelly later said that she had sought to emulate Chastain's iconic sports bra moment in tribute. Men have often removed their shirts in celebration. The uncovering of the sports bra, however, brought the act a special significance: a subversive one. It is this subversion that is the focus of our book.

A woman celebrating and uncovering her powerful, athletic body in such a carefree, spontaneous moment was revolutionary in 1999 and remains revolutionary today. The vast majority of our cultural examples of women's physicality being celebrated on world stages have been more about what a woman's body looks like, and who it could serve, than what her body can do and achieve. An exemplar of the former would be beauty pageants such as the Miss

World competition. While we have for the most part moved beyond those contests, with their popularity and place within popular culture having waned considerably, the fact that they were until very recently the epitome of what women could achieve outside of motherhood (the only more important vocation a woman could have) speaks volumes. It has only been in very recent years that women have started being recognized and celebrated for their intellect and abilities, rather than their looks, conformity to feminine ideals and capacity for reproduction. We have a long way to go, however, with women's physicality still being seen as inferior to men's. This is a central concern of our book.

Patriarchy, sexism and sport

It is within this context that we discuss the truly revolutionary nature of Chastain's and Kelly's celebratory acts. Women have rarely been able to celebrate their embodiment in such an unfettered manner on the world stage. And to do so in sport, traditionally the preserve of men's dominant physicality, is subversion in action. Culturally, sport is to men what beauty pageants are to women, in terms of enforcing and re-enforcing gender roles. The history of sport, from the ancient to the modern Olympics, tells the story of an activity designed to promote, affirm and reinforce men's physicality. While men have always been able to participate and compete in sport, developing and marking their physical being in games and competitions designed by men for men, women were gatekept out. This gatekeeping happened in a variety of ways and for a variety of reasons.

Beyond simply not allowing women to participate through both rules and social ostracization, women were gaslit by the medical and sporting establishment, who designated them too fragile for rigorous physical exercise. Indeed, doctors themselves feared that women's uteruses may fall out if they played sport. The founder of the modern Olympics, Pierre de Coubertin, said not only that 'the true Olympic hero is the individual male adult,' and 'I feel that the Olympic Games must be reserved for men,' but, to be entirely explicit, 'as to the admission of women to the Games, I remain strongly against it. It was against my will that they were admitted to a growing number of competitions' and 'add a female element, and the event becomes monstrous.' Even the English Football Association (the FA) stated in 1921 that the sport was quite simply 'unsuitable for females and ought not be encouraged'.[1] Social roles were made clear: a man is allowed to be physical, thus paving the way for his physical dominance, and a woman is not, making her passive and subordinate. It should come to us as no surprise, then, that if we take this into account, sport doesn't simply reflect gendered differences but creates them. Sport, used in this way, is a tool to uphold the myth of male dominance and female subordination. Seeing Chastain's and Kelly's celebrations in this light helps us to understand why their representation matters so much. These moments, over twenty years apart, are reflective of a much bigger cultural phenomenon: the mounting challenge to patriarchal control.

What do we mean by patriarchy? On the whole, we are seeking to avoid as much jargon and as many technical terms as possible. But the notion of patriarchy is one that we simply cannot ignore or avoid since it has proven to be the key determinant in what *Women's Sport* is. We will, therefore, be referring to patriarchy frequently throughout this book. In the broadest terms, in which we follow the likes of Kate Manne (philosopher at Cornell

University) and Angela Saini (science journalist and author), we take patriarchy to be a system, some would say social structure, that upholds men's power, dominance and privilege over women and other marginalized groups of people. It justifies this power with sexism and polices it with misogyny. Patriarchy embodies an ideology of male supremacism, one which informs our social and personal arrangements, setting up unequal power relations and baking them into our laws, our institutions and our cultural practices. Like other social structures, while it has been created by us, it is now beyond the control of any one individual. Men might gain some benefits from it, since it reserves for them certain privileges. According to our account, however, patriarchy harms men as well, even though it harms women (and non-binary, trans and queer people) even more. Feminism opposes patriarchy since the central feminist commitment, as we see it, is that people should be equal irrespective of their genders. Indeed, because we see the imposition of a strict gender binary as a central pillar of patriarchy, we want to articulate our feminism as a view that includes everyone, especially those who do not conform to the binary. In that case, instead of saying only that men and women should be equal, we can simply say that *everyone* ought to be equal in all significant respects. There is a lot more to this view of feminism, and *Feminist Sport*, which we will be explaining during the course of the book, but we already have enough to set definitions aside and proceed.

Sportswear

Women's sport has a long and troubled history with its sportswear. Women's sportswear and bodies are either: 1) hypersexualized (as we see with mandatory revealing outfits in beach volleyball, tennis and gymnastics, for example – outfits which are more for the male gaze than performance); 2) castigated as unfeminine (such as women who play rugby and football, seen as unsexy 'butch lesbians' to the heterosexual gaze, and Black women and Women of Colour who are seen as 'too masculine' and are policed from competing under the guise of 'unfairness'); or 3) erased completely (such as hijab-wearing women who play sport, and Black women who swim but who don't have access to or are banned from wearing sportswear – unfamiliar to the White gaze – that would be appropriate for their participation). It seems that no matter what a woman in sport wears or does, she will always be judged.

The reaction to Chloe Kelly celebrating in her sports bra is revealing of something larger, in exactly the same way in which Morocco's Nouhaila Benzina wearing her hijab while playing in the 2023 Football World Cup is: the focus is on her choice of clothing, rather than her football performance. And this focus reflects the underlying social message that women shouldn't be seen participating in public life. Women's bodies being policed in sport is a powerful tool of patriarchal control. It is important to recognize that this is part of a much longer history of keeping women in their place, and that this is an added barrier that women in sport face in a way that men just don't. Journalist Shireen Ahmed writes that, whether a woman chooses to wear a 'bikini, a burkini, or a burka', she is part of the same feminist struggle: her participation in everyday life is being policed.[2] Policing what women athletes wear and how they wear it is part of the gendered environment that makes sport unwelcoming for girls and women, and this has lifelong consequences for participation in physical activity. We may think that we are beyond this, as of this work's publication in 2025, but negative reactions to Kelly's and Benzina's defiant acts show that we still have a very long way to go. Much has been written about Chastain's celebration in particular, with initial media reactions focusing on the act as being disrespectful and even vulgar, blaming her for taking the focus away from the football itself by baring her bra. The truth was that the public wasn't ready for this. However, it was never about the bra, as the title of Chastain's later autobiography reminds us.[3] A woman revealing herself on her terms, and doing so in a sports bra, was emblematic of so much more. A lesson in liberation.

Brassieres, or bras, have long been the subject of feminist analysis and action. Indeed, bra-burning is practically synonymous with 1960s and '70s feminism. Of this corner of the feminist struggle, bell hooks writes in *Feminism Is for Everybody*:

> Looking back after years of feeling comfortable choosing whether or not to wear a bra, I can remember what a momentous decision this was thirty years ago. Women stripping their bodies of unhealthy and uncomfortable, restrictive clothing – bras, girdles, corsets, garter belts, etc. – was a ritualistic, radical reclaiming of the health and glory of the female body.[4]

Various garments have been used historically to support and cover, and sometimes to reveal or emphasize, women's breasts. Often understood as an instrument of patriarchy, the main purpose of the bra, in patriarchal societies, is concealment and control. This is because women's bodies have long been considered sites of transgression. Indeed, a biblical passage states, 'Sin began with a woman, and we must all die because of her' (Ecclesiasticus 25:24). And precisely because breasts have long been considered a symbol of fertility and reproduction, when not being used for those purposes they had to be covered up so as not to inspire sin. Ironically, in concealing the breasts, bras simultaneously emphasize them: the classic Madonna/Whore bind.

Sports bras, on the other hand, are an undergarment designed for function and freedom rather than concealment and control. The modern sports bra was designed by three women, Lisa Lindahl, Hinda Miller and Polly Smith, and patented in the United States in 1979. Described by the Smithsonian National Museum of American History as an invention that 'actually made sports possible', the sports bra is a feminist tool: not only one that is a practical method for making sports participation possible and comfortable for people with breasts, but one that has become a symbol for so much more. Sports bras have nothing to do with restraining women or emphasizing/controlling their femininity, but rather actively release women from constraints: of their bodies and of society. The sports bra exposes the truth that our bodies were never the constraint in the first place; patriarchy was.[5]

It is no coincidence that it was in this performance garment that Chastain and Kelly celebrated their winning goals twenty and forty-three years later, respectively. Understanding the weight of this cultural symbolism thus helps us to understand the major public hand-wringing about whether a woman's (sports) bra could be exposed to the public at large. The exposure brought the sporting woman to public attention in a way that subverted what we had been taught to think about her. This act blatantly transgressed our expectations of what a woman was 'allowed' to show in public, and reframed how we saw her: for her athleticism and joy rather than her role in the patriarchal order.

In a world in which women's bodies are routinely hyper-sexualized, and girls and women are regularly (explicitly and implicitly) slut-shamed when they transgress the received codes of sexual conduct, Chastain and Kelly refused the social contract and rewrote the book. It was *her* body and *her* goal. She was entitled to glory in both. In the act of celebrating in this way – in the exact same manner as her men's football counterparts do – she was casting off stereotypes and expectations. This act was decidedly *not* for patriarchal ends. This is what was challenging, indeed subversive, about the celebration. As journalist Deborah Linton wrote in *British Vogue*, Kelly's act was 'a lesson in liberation'.[6]

Thousands of miles away from Britain, across the Atlantic, sits another site of women's sports bra symbolism. The Sports Bra in Portland, Oregon, is the first sports bar in the world to be dedicated solely to women's sport. Speaking to Upworthy website, owner Jenny Nguyen said: 'At first, I thought that The Bra would just be a place to celebrate women in sports but now I see that it's uplifted girls in so many different ways.'[7] We take the sports bra, in this book, as both a symbol and tool of liberation.

Taking sport for women seriously

England beat Germany in that Euro 2022 final in which Kelly removed her shirt, a result that had a wider significance in a country that had struggled to take women's football, and all women's sport, seriously. Women had been banned from playing FA-sanctioned football in the United Kingdom until as recently as 1972 (a ban that started in 1921, when women's games could draw 50,000-strong crowds: a feat we only began seeing again in 2022). Starting from scratch after a fifty-year ban, the so-called 'women's game' had to overcome multiple further disadvantages to reach this point in which almost all football fans were watching, cheering on and taking this team of Lionesses to their hearts. There had been virtually no funding, no investment, no facilities, no expertise, no media coverage. The England national team manager from 1998 to 2013, Hope Powell, was for a while having to take the team kit home and wash it herself for the next game. With such a lack of resources in the sport, there was no prospect of professionalism for quite some time, with even the country's best players having to train part-time after working their day jobs. Only gradually did the possibilities of women's football dawn on the governing bodies. And when England was awarded the hosting of the 2022 Euro tournament a plan was put in place to turn the team into genuine contenders. The top coach was appointed. Sarina Wiegman had won the previous competition with her home country the Netherlands, regularly pitting her tactics against men counterparts, who coached the other national sides, and showing that she could out-think them. The FA granted use of its best available facilities for preparation during the eighteen months leading up to the event.

Chloe Kelly was one of several stars. England won the European title well, defeating several of the top teams along the way. Football fans of all stripes saw the brilliant skills of Beth Mead and Alessia Russo, the latter scoring the most remarkable goal of the tournament in a semi-final demolition of Sweden, with a backheel that would henceforth be known as The Russo. Interest in the side's fortunes gathered momentum as Norway, coached by a man, were utterly obliterated 8–0 by Sarina's tactical system, and then one of the favourites, Spain (a team, it turns out, beset by misogynistic problems in the changing room, as we will later discuss), were beaten in the quarter-final by Georgia Stanway's extra-time rocket (Spain would get revenge a year later in the 2023 World Cup). Fans who had disparaged the women's game, judging it an inferior product while at the same time lamenting the perennial failures of the England men's side, saw here a team of genuine winners. Earps, Williamson, Bronze, Toone, Bright, Daly, White, Hemp and Kirby, along with all the others, became household names. Keira Walsh controlled the midfield during most matches, and was recognized as one of the most tactically astute and influential players of England's win. Before Kelly's winner, Ella Toone had herself scored with an incredible, spectacular lobbed goal that will always be remembered. Not many players, of any gender, could have taken that chance with such composure and flawless execution.

As the English nation celebrated, commentators and pundits were already recognizing the significance of this moment for women in football and for women's place in society generally. It was dawning on the country in football women were as good as men. Indeed, in this moment, they were even better. Traditional football fans were scratching their heads, waking up to the realization that until now they had been watching only half the football. Women's club sides up and down the country received an immediate boost, with season ticket sales increasing sixfold in some cases. Former England player Alex Scott, who had played through many of those difficult early days, and was now a pundit for the BBC's coverage, emotionally articulated this moment of revolution:

> This is a dream for every young girl playing football. This is incredible. It's not just me, there are so many people that have been involved in getting women's football to

this point, to see this team lift this trophy. I can't even sum it up. This is literally what we have all been waiting [for] and dreaming of. The amount of investment that has gone into the games to get it to this point. Do you know what this moment reminds me of? '99 Women's World Cup when USA won that. It changed the face of soccer in America forever. I feel it . . . in England . . . this is that moment. Let's just remind ourselves as well, back in 2018, we were begging people to host in their stadiums a women's game for this Euro. So many people said no. I hope you are all looking at yourselves right now because you weren't brave enough to see what it could have been.[8]

In 2023 the Women's Football World Cup inspired the same revelation among the masses in joint host countries Aotearoa New Zealand and Australia. Scenes of the Australian Matildas' epic twenty-penalty shoot-out win over France, in a sell-out stadium crowd of nearly 50,000, were broadcast to Australia's biggest television audience of 2023, pushing back the nightly news and being streamed live in stadiums around the country, where men's sports were being played simultaneously, but with attention elsewhere.

This vast and inspiring deep well of interest in women's football is echoed around the world. Brazil changed work hours via a national ordinance so that fans could watch the games. A record 53.9 million viewers in China watched the country's 6–1 defeat to England during the group stages. For the first time ever, three African teams – South Africa, Morocco and Nigeria – made the knock-out stage. The groundswell was palpable. On TikTok young women were sharing how their new-found love of sport was a revelation. Beyond National level, women's club-level football was and is also seeing its own surge of fan interest and growth. FC Barcelona Femení twice broke their crowd records in 2022, with an all-time high of 91,648 fans at the Camp Nou against Wolfsburg. Arsenal Women did the same in 2023 and again in early 2024, when they sold out Emirates Stadium twice in succession. The revolution was here.

A global revolution?

But is this truly a revolution for women's sport? Would the effects of the success be long-lasting, and could they transfer to other sports, and to other countries, where women have universally struggled for the same recognition and opportunities in sport that men get? Or will women's sport never attain the same status as men's because it will always be somehow inferior? In this book, we are considering what sport could be, if we had a more just society. And we are distinguishing between *Women's Sport*, henceforth in italics, as it currently is – a creation of the existing patriarchal order – and sport played by women. These two things need not be the same. In particular, we are looking at what a feminist vision of sport would and should be, a vision that puts the interests of women and queer people at the centre while at the same time showing that those interests align with the interests of us all. The rise of this new inclusive sport, which we will call *Feminist Sport* to distinguish it from the old order, can be a portal through which we all win.

Our view might be considered by many to be challenging, counter-intuitive and difficult. This is because we take a number of accepted orthodoxies that surround human bodies and sport to be false. Furthermore, many conventional views concerning what is best for women in sport (and beyond) are misplaced, often following an agenda that is decided by men and sold to women as being in their best interests. There are some who will find it impossible to accept our interpretation of *Women's Sport*. Others, with a particular feminist background, should find our account entirely conducive to their goals. We recognize, nevertheless, that feminist thinking has been co-opted into such a broad range of views that almost anyone can now profess to be a feminist. Indeed, it is not unknown to find appeals to feminism, and the supposed best interests of women, now being invoked in essentially oppressive projects that ultimately seek to keep women in their place, serving traditional gendered roles and patriarchal ends.

Our arguments are unlikely to sway anyone who has already inadvertently fallen down that alt-right rabbit hole. But there are many others – women, men and beyond – faithfully believed by us to be the great majority, who have no firm views on this topic, are yet to give it serious consideration and are willing to approach the issues with an open mind. It is these readers for whom this book is intended, with the hope that they will come to question and reject some of the received wisdom. Indeed, we aim to deal a fatal blow to certain ways of thinking about women's bodies and women in sport: those ways of thinking that emphasize the frailty, delicateness and, not to put too fine a point on it, physical inferiority of women compared to men. Once accepted, this pernicious view of women justifies the claim that *Women's Sport* will never be the match of men's, perhaps that women should not even participate in sport, or at least not in some sports, and that if they do, they need to be protected so as not to put their own bodies at risk. This pernicious view also upholds the strict gender binary.

The basic argument

Our basic argument in this book can now be introduced. Later chapters will fill out the detail behind these claims and explain some of the implications.

A way into the issues is the sporting performance gap that is sometimes alleged to exist between men and women. Some estimates from sport scientists (which we believe to be flawed) place this at roughly 10 per cent. This estimation is drawn from world records, which historically generally show a 10 per cent gap between men's and women's performances. The idea, then, is that men will always be able to run 10 per cent faster than women, jump 10 per cent higher, be 10 per cent stronger, and so on. Furthermore, this difference is considered 'natural' and we are told stems ultimately from our differences in biology. Perhaps men have evolved for their athleticism, for hunting or warring, whereas women have evolved for their child-rearing and caring. The former traits tend to greater success in sports than the latter traits. But we will leave the details of such a natural history to those who actually believe this wisdom, which we do not.

Other tenets follow from this belief in the essential biological differences of men and women concerning the arrangements we make for sport. The foremost of these tenets is that we need a gender division in sport, where men compete only against men and women compete only against women. There are at least two justifications for this. One is fairness, since it is alleged that women would never win sporting contests if they were obliged to compete against men. The other justification is athlete protection, since men, being so much (10 per cent?) more powerful than women, could thereby endanger them in direct sporting contests and, in contact sports, cause women serious harm. These views construe *Women's Sport* as a protected space that must be guarded against unwarranted and unwanted entry. Women, being physically inferior according to this account, need this protected space so that they can flourish within it, sometimes winning, and doing so safely and fairly. Sport is sex-separated, they say, primarily, if not wholly, for the benefit of women. On the biological difference view, the superiority of men is taken for granted, understood as both natural and inevitable, and has resulted in a response that is represented as well-meaning, just and serving the best interests of women.

We accept none of the above. In patriarchal societies, which almost all of ours are, social arrangements, including sporting arrangements, are constructed in service of the masters rather than the oppressed. When governing bodies, predominantly ruled by men, uphold the sex-separation of sport, this should be taken as a good indicator that it is designed to serve not the interests of women but of men. How so?

Once sex-separated on a strict binary basis, the performance difference between men and women becomes reinforced and exaggerated. Sex-segregation, which is how we see it, creates and constantly recreates the supposed differences between men and women as an important supporting pillar of patriarchy. To understand how, let us approach this first by way of an analogy. It is clear that a division can be made among most societies into those who are poor and those who are rich. Once people are divided along these lines of wealth, we see how economic arrangements can reproduce and exaggerate rather than reduce the initial difference. For example, the poor are frequently asked to pay a higher unit-rate for the household energy they consume, since they are more likely to be put on prepayment meters, which charge more. There are many other bills, such as insurances and services, where the less wealthy cannot afford the discounted annual fee and so pay instead a monthly instalment that overall works out as more. Those who are rich can afford to buy many other goods in bulk, at a discounted rate. There are also many mechanisms that effectively ensure that the very rich pay proportionally less in taxes than those on moderate incomes. And with cash liquidity, the rich can invest in their networking, training and education in a way that the poor usually cannot. Education, if it is not freely available to all, becomes a key driver of inequality. Once the economic conditions have positioned you as rich, you will be treated one way; once they have positioned you as poor, you will be treated a different way. The division becomes entrenched and reified: made real. The board game Monopoly illustrates all of this. Owning a majority of the assets will make you richer and richer as you drain the cash from your 'poorer' opponents until they are bankrupt.

Now let us return to sport and how its participants are divided into men and women. Once there are these two groups, the possibility of them being treated differently exists and, in a world dominated by men, through the ideology of male supremacism, or patriarchy, it is unsurprising to find that *Women's Sport* gets treated less well. *Women's Sport* is hugely underfunded compared to men's. Consequently, the facilities are not as good. Women have less opportunity to devote themselves to their sport full time. The prizes are not as attractive as the men's, either in terms of money or status. The TV deals put less cash into *Women's Sport* than into men's *Sport*. The broadcasters might say that *Women's Sport* is a relatively inferior product, so it doesn't deserve equal finances. But is such a difference produced by the relative lack of funding or a justification of it? We say the former.

Indeed, our view is that if there is any performance gap, of 10 per cent or any other extent, this is caused by the differential treatment of women in sport rather than stemming from a putative natural biological difference. Just as we can identify mechanisms by which a division into rich and poor is then exacerbated, so a division into men's and women's sport leads only to an increase in any such disparities. One might think it somewhat surprising that the performance gap between men and women is estimated at *only* 10 per cent given that the difference in funding between the two sports is far greater than that. For example, in the final year in which Cristiano Ronaldo played in the men's Premier League in English football, his annual salary was greater than the combined annual salaries of all the players in the equivalent Women's Super League. All of the players! It is somewhat remarkable that women's performances get as close to men's as they do, given disparities of this extent.

Let us be clear what these financial differences entail. It is not simply that greater salaries for men mean that they try harder and become more dedicated to their sport. Most athletes are likely motivated by sporting success, and the financial rewards of that success are only secondary. It is more the concrete, practical matters that follow from relative lack of funding, other than player salaries, that have an effect on performance. We recently visited a second-tier football club that had both a men's team and a women's team. The women, we learnt, were not allowed to train on the men's practice pitch, since the club did not want the surface damaged through overuse. The men's needs had priority. Women instead had to train on an artificial surface since, of the other pitches available, this was the only one that had floodlights. This itself was necessary since the women had to train in the evenings, after work, given that the club paid the women only part-time salaries and many of the players had day jobs. This pattern of access was repeated. Women were allowed strength and conditioning training only when the men were not using the gym. Their relative lack of importance was signalled in other ways. They were not allowed use of the players' lounge at the training site since that was for the men only. The changing rooms for the women were surprisingly small. Indeed, if more than a dozen players were needing to change for training, it was hard to see where they would all fit, and they would probably have to use the communal showers in three or four shifts. The fitness coach was a part-time intern who was also studying at the local university. We suspect that this was actually one of the better organized and more progressive clubs, which had decided to support and build its women's side, but it was clear that this team was secondary, by some distance, to the men's team, which was still very much seen as the core business of the organization.

There are other models. Some clubs have decided to have only a women's team, and one reason to do so could be that, as long as there are both men's and women's teams taking resources from the same pot, the men will always get by far the larger share. Instead, we could give women their own pot. This does not solve the problem, however, since, to pursue the metaphor, the pot they are given is likely to be smaller than the pot a men-only club would get. The problem of unequal resourcing is reflected at a higher level, often stemming from broadcasting revenues, which go predominantly to men's sport. Even in tennis, where the governing body for the women's game split from the men's governing body, comparable rights sales have not been negotiated. One might say that until women's tennis is as good as men's, broadcasters shouldn't have to pay as much for the rights. But this is a somewhat different attitude to men's sports in which broadcasters saw the opportunity of coverage and paid the money that became effectively an investment in the development of the sport, with a subsequent raising of standards. With Grand Slam organizers still generally offering lower prize money to women than to men, this itself creates the impression of a lesser form of the sport, which even on its own is a reason to put viewers off.

The division along gender lines is not, of course, unique in sport. Perhaps it could be said that it merely reflects a division among human beings, and other biological species, that we accept as real and a proper basis for different treatment. Nevertheless, we will argue that the division in sport and beyond is of particular importance to patriarchy since it not only preserves but actually helps create and recreate the dogma of both the binary and of natural male dominance. It is also notable, however, that many other divisions along the lines of gender have been rejected. We no longer think of men's occupations and women's occupations, for instance. Of course, it is still a reality that some jobs are dominated by one gender, but it is rare that anyone would justify this as natural and desirable even if it is a socioeconomic fact. Employment law and cultural changes have helped us overcome some parts of the traditional thinking. For instance, even if, which we find doubtful, men on average made better local government managers than women, there is a widespread acceptance that when appointing to such a role, one should always appoint the best candidate, irrespective of gender. The best candidate could still be a woman even if men on average had an advantage since one is not, after all, appointing an average candidate but a particular best one. This has helped break down a sexual division of labour in some countries. But note that similar considerations have not been applied in sport, in which the gender division is still applied rigidly, even if not unproblematically (see Chapter Three). If the best tennis player in all the world were a woman, she would not be in competition with the men, supposedly because men on average are physically superior to women. As we will go on to argue (in Chapter Five), this suggests that *Women's Sport* is not a protected space at all but, rather, a segregated space. This difference in terminology is important, since a *protected* space serves the best interests of the disadvantaged party in an unequal relationship, whereas a *segregated* space serves the interests of the dominant party.

In order to overcome that suggestion, the defender of sex-segregated sport will again invoke the idea of the natural superiority of men, so we should resume the argument concerning this. We have presented the alternative viewpoint in which, once sport is divided along any lines, and in this case gender, it allows for the possibility that the divided groups are treated unequally, to the benefit of one and hindrance of the other. This is what we indeed argue and defend the view that the sexual division of sport helps create the alleged 10 per cent performance advantage of men over women rather than the sexual division being justified by a pre-existing performance advantage.

At this point, an opponent may well say that such a view is absurd since, irrespective of any contribution that differences in funding and facilities could make, men will always be bigger, stronger and faster than women. No matter what our organizational arrangements are, it will be said, men come out as superior and, as before, we will always have to sex-segregate sport for women's own benefit. In one respect, there could be some truth in this argument but only because the organization of sport itself is unlikely on its own to restore the physical equality of men and women. The reason for this, however, is that there are wider social and cultural determinants of why men are bigger than women and these are outside the control of sport even though they are reflected within it. That said, we hold that sport plays a major role in reinforcing this difference (see Chapter Two) and argue that only by allowing women to occasionally beat men do we provide the conditions for this becoming normalized: a future possibility that patriarchy violently resists.

Biology is not destiny

What we have to accept is that most societies are sexually differentiated environments in which we grow up responding and reacting to expectations along gender lines. This begins *in utero* or at birth, where we are classified as male or female, and persists over our lifetimes. There are rewards for satisfying gendered norms and penalties for disappointing them. On their own, genes do very little. Chromosomes code for proteins and there are many intermediate stages between a person's genotype and their phenotypes: between their DNA and their observable physical features, such as their height. Hence, it is coded into regular human DNA that we grow legs but the legs that we grow also require environmental inputs to be what they are. A child unluckily born on a space station, weightless in zero gravity, would not develop legs of the extent and strength of our Earth-bound legs since muscle growth requires the exercise afforded by a resistance against weight. Our physical features are a result of environment just as much as genetics, which means that biology most certainly is not destiny. Indeed, what we recognize today as a persistent gender binary is merely a classification designed by humans, such as race or caste is.

What sort of environmental factors might explain the average physical differences between men and women? We have seen that post-Second World War improvements in diet and nutrition have, in a relatively short period of time, increased average heights in many societies. People are much bigger now, not because their genes have changed, but because people have fed their bodies more and better. Suppose one were to say that while men and women have increased in height in recent decades, men have always stayed, on average, taller than women, so this suggests an underlying genetic predisposition to physical superiority. The problem with this is that it assumes that there are no other environmental determinants of physical traits. There are, however, cultural determinants that work, in part, by ensuring that women stay smaller than men by ensuring less food, poorer nutrition and less physical activity.

Here is a story that explains how this can work. Neighbours have children at the same time. At birth, one is assigned as a boy and one is assigned as a girl. The differences begin immediately. The boy is fed all he wants and is indeed praised for feeding a lot, even if this is more than he needs. The girl, however, is given just what she needs and no more (there is evidence of differential nutrition intakes even with breastfeeding). As the boy grows, he is praised for being big and strong and encouraged to become more so. He should eat a lot and exercise, playing rough and tumble with his father while still in short trousers. If he has a predisposition towards being big, he is encouraged to think of this as a possible sporting advantage: making of it an asset. The girl instead is praised for being pretty and passive, her skirts getting in the way of rigorous play. She risks becoming unloved or a social outcast if she grows too large. Above all, she does not want to be judged fat. Being large has no societal upside for girls. The boy becomes a man, encouraged to develop physically and participate in sports. He is proud if he can eat an oversized juicy steak at a barbecue. He can fight and defend his partner and family, if needed. The woman, in contrast, would be socially castigated if she were to eat a whole steak to herself. She is encouraged to share the meat with others and eat more salads and other low-calorie options for the good of her figure. She would never be expected to engage in physical combat, even if it is playful. Rather, one of the most disturbing sights for society to see would be two women in a fight. This is a story only, but a plausible one: almost all of us will have experienced something like it, growing up. There is evidence that, on average, men's daily calorie intake exceeds women's by a significant degree. Is this due to different genetic instincts for food? It seems to suggest so when we see different 'recommended' daily calorie intakes for men and women. What might be a cultural product is thereby presented as a natural state. Need it be so?

Further advances in food technology, and more, have exaggerated the physical differences between men and women even further. There is now a wide availability of protein powders that will build muscle bulk. Other than medical usage, these protein supplements are taken almost exclusively by men. Again, this is not because of a natural urge for protein shakes. Rather, there are men who want to be big, whereas very few women do. As the 2008 film *Bigger, Stronger, Faster* details, there are many men who are willing to go a step beyond supplements and inject with anabolic steroids, resulting in gigantically enhanced muscle bulk that looks decidedly unnatural. Relatively few women resort to these methods. Women are encouraged to turn to calorie-controlled smoothies to become physically smaller. There are, of course, women bodybuilders who do develop a pronounced musculature, but note the different responses that these women receive. Society is in awe of the men's muscles but disconcerted and bemused, if not repelled, by the women's. Society loves a small woman. The differing gendered expectations mean that gyms are often designed to suit men, since men are supposed to be big and women are supposed to be petite, delicate and fragrant.

Cultural expectations

The suggestion here, then, is that the physical differences between men and women are manufactured by a culture of different expectations and treatments that apply from birth and endure throughout lifetimes of development. Chloe Kelly's celebratory exposure of her upper body, clad only in her sports bra, showed defiance in the face of such expectations. Women are not supposed to take pride in having a strong, athletic, physical body. If they must have one, they had best hide it, and they should certainly not show off their sports bra shamelessly, as if it's the most natural thing in the world to do. Has she no shame? No, she hasn't. And rightly so.

It is these gender-differentiated cultural expectations that ultimately explain the different treatments of men's and women's sports too. They explain, for instance, why different kinds of training facilities are thought appropriate for men and women. A viral

TikTok from American basketball player Sedona Prince in 2021 exposed how an NCAA (National Collegiate Athletic Association) basketball meet treated the men and women competitors differently.[9] The men's teams were given access to a huge gymnasium with all manner of high-tech weight-training equipment. In contrast, women were shown to a small set of dumbbells set aside in one corner for their use. The differences didn't end there. The men and women were offered different kinds of food: protein for the men, salads for the women. Even when competitors were given welcome gifts, the men got a 500-piece jigsaw puzzle and the women's puzzle was only 150 pieces. Less is expected of women, reinforcing their smallness.

Of course, this might seem one local example, and there is plenty of open misogyny to be found in the United States. But even well-meaning supporters of women's sports can fall into the trap of treating women differently. A new training centre has been planned at La Trobe University in Melbourne for the Australian women's national football team, the Matildas, but, again, with less emphasis on weight training than the men would get. It has been billed as 'designed by women for women', but the emphasis has been placed on cardiovascular training (treadmills and the like) rather than weight training (strength and conditioning): another lesson in expectations for women to be thin rather than bulky, in 'good shape' rather than strong, even when they are elite athletes. Sporting interventions designed for women too easily become designed for *the expectations* put on women: for smaller goals. The danger is that those expectations then create the reality. Women's training shoes are narrower than men's, for example, but is this because women's feet are narrower or does it make women's feet narrower? Diets tailored for women athletes present a similar danger. Hence, while the men drink their protein shakes, women get 'period smoothies', full of 'vitamins' so as to compensate for the 'physical strain and trauma' of menstruation, but containing relatively little protein. The men then get bigger and the women are left behind.

Different expectations and treatments of women, both inside and outside of sport, conspire to create their physical differences rather than being a response to them. Essentially, we have here what philosophers will call a Euthyphro question. This happens when two things occur together but we need to understand the order of explanation or dependence between them. The original question, in Plato, concerned whether the gods love certain things because they are good, or whether those things are good because the gods love them. In the case of women's physicality, we can consider the question: are women treated differently because they are the physical inferiors of men, or are women the physical inferiors of men because they are treated differently? The 'naturalist' position, with which we started, favours the former answer, justifying the differential treatment of women, within their so-called protected space, because they are inferior to men, could never win against them and would be unsafe competing with them. But we favour the latter view, in which the physical differences between men and women are created – socially constructed – rather than natural.

The latter is also what we take to be the true feminist response to the Euthyphro question, despite many recent supporters of naturalism branding themselves as feminists. But we have a number of important feminists on our side, for instance philosopher Simone de Beauvoir, who stated that 'One is not born, but rather becomes, woman.'[10] One becomes (or is made) a woman over time, by being forced to accept a position within a patriarchal structure and satisfying the expectations regarding how one looks and behaves: what we can call the gender norms. A woman who rejects these norms is, herself, rejected by society. Being a woman is, then, not simply a reflection of what sex organs one has. Angela Saini has recently emphasized that it is not women but patriarchy itself that is fragile, as evidenced by the fact that it must constantly recreate itself and, somewhat paradoxically, constantly reassert its putative immutable nature in biology. As Saini says: 'By thinking about gendered inequality as rooted in something unalterable within us, we fail to see it for what it is: something more fragile that has had to be constantly remade and reasserted. We're in the process of remaking it even now.'[11]

We have already conceded that our claims might be considered controversial since they overturn much accepted thinking concerning women's relationship with sport and their physical being generally. Women are routinely thought of as the 'weaker sex', but we think this gets matters wrong in a number of ways. There is nothing natural about women's physical inferiority. Indeed, we argue, along with Beauvoir and Saini, that it is far from clear that women are, as a matter of fact, physically inferior to men. That all depends on what you mean by physical inferiority – the criteria for this are usually chosen by men. As Saini points out in her 2017 book *Inferior*, women tend to live longer than men and have better rates of recovery from major illnesses. Women are the strongest in at least these respects. But as well as that point of dispute, the division between, and then the differential treatment of, men and women must be ongoing, constant and policed if it is to remain in place. It is patriarchy that is surprisingly fragile, not women. In the chapters to follow, we will calculate some of the implications of this view of women's physical being, especially what it means for women's place in sport. We will also, by the end, trouble the very idea that a binary consisting only of men and women exists at all.

We have set out the argument that we are going to develop and detail in the rest of this book. The differences between men and women that we see reflected in their relative sporting performances, we believe, are not natural in any immutable sense but are created by our organizational arrangements and a wider social culture of differing gendered expectations. Boys are encouraged to be big and strong while girls are stigmatized if they become so. The physical being of anyone other than men is diminished. This upholds patriarchy: a system of sex-based unequal power, dominance and privilege. In such a context, a woman succeeding in sport is an act of subversion.

2

Sport Is a Feminist Issue

In 1902 Florence Madeline 'Madge' Syers, a British athlete, entered the World Figure Skating Championships and would go on to win second place. What was remarkable about this feat was not her silver medal, but rather that she – a woman – was competing at all. Up until that point, while skating as a pastime was popular among men and women, international competitions existed for men only. Madge entered the World Championships regardless, exploiting a loophole in the competition rules which did not explicitly state that women *couldn't* participate. While she faced calls for her to be banned, including from the judges themselves, Madge competed anyway, challenging the dominant ideology of the time that considered sport unsuitable for women and thus taking up the mantle of feminist killjoy.

Philosopher Sara Ahmed, author of *The Feminist Killjoy Handbook*, describes the feminist killjoy as someone who 'gets in the way', just as Madge did in entering a space which was not meant for her. At a time when sport was considered an activity only men took part in, and women were thought too fragile for rigorous physical pursuits, Madge's participation was a revolutionary act. Madge's athletic career is thus one of refusing the status quo:

You become a feminist killjoy when you are not willing to go along with something, to get along with someone, sitting there quietly taking it all in. You become a feminist killjoy when you react, speak back, to those with authority, using words like *sexism* because this is what you hear. There is so much you are supposed to avoid saying or doing in order not to ruin an occasion. Another dinner ruined, so many dinners ruined![1]

Women in sport have ruined many dinners. Entering spaces and competitions and boardrooms that had been special enclaves set apart for men only, women have always taken up space and demanded change in and through sport. While today we can sometimes find ourselves thinking it almost unfathomable that women once didn't have a league of their own, in this chapter we tell the stories of the hidden figures of women in sport who fought to be included, and the story of how *Women's Sport* emerged. Tracing not only historical examples of the feminist killjoy in sport but contemporary ones too, we show the history of women (and all marginalized people, including Black people, People of Colour, disabled people and queer people) in sport to be part of a larger feminist lineage, positioning sport as a feminist issue. We offer this as an act of recovering feminist history, turning their battles 'into a source of strength as well as an inspiration'.[2]

In the wake of Madge Syers's participation, the International Skating Union (ISU) was forced to grapple with the 'issue' of women's participation. In the debate around this question at the time, three primary concerns were raised: '(1) the dress prevents the judges from seeing the feet; (2) a judge might judge a girl to whom he was attached; and (3) it is difficult to compare women with men.'[3] Madge confronted all three. She scandalously shortened her dresses to reveal her ankles, and her performance spoke for itself on counts two and three. Indeed, T. D. Richardson, a fellow skater and judge, later wrote: 'Rumour, nay more than rumour – a good deal of expert opinion – thought she should have won.'[4] Madge Syers showed the world that women could not only compete with men but win too. Ultimately, however, in 1903 the ISU banned women from competing after a vote of 6–3.

All was not lost, though. In 1905 the ISU created a new women's competition: the Ladies' Championship. Madge would go on to win these competitions in 1906 and 1907 and would become the women's Olympic Champion in 1908 (the first time Figure Skating was included in the Olympics). Madge Syers created an incredible and groundbreaking legacy for women in sport, forging a path that had not existed before.

This easy inspirational legacy narrative doesn't tell the whole story, however. A feminist killjoy never simply accepts the status quo, and in the spirit of Madge herself we must critically place what happened after 1902 into a much larger context: that of the splitting of *Women's Sport* from *Sport*. We argue that rather than being a feminist win, this creation of the ladies' category was a patriarchal response. In this chapter we explain how and why.

We will show that where women were first included in sport (or where they simply included themselves, as Madge did), it was only once they started threatening men's dominance and entitlement that they were separated into their own category. We thus tell the story of how *Women's Sport* was created and now still exists as a socially subordinate category because women started challenging the myth of men's physical superiority, and in doing so challenged the patriarchal narrative that biology is destiny with regard to sport and beyond. These women show that women were never 'too fragile' for sport, but actually can and do win. And then when they did win, women were usually relegated to a new category not long after: that of *Women's Sport*. This new category was one over which the 'old boys club', in charge of sport, could assert control, and through years of under-investment, lack of support and outright sabotage could make and remake as the inferior class. In doing so, they reasserted patriarchal domination. The long-term effect was that, decades later, patriarchal sexism and misogyny would have seeded, sprouted and cultivated the extremely persistent myth of women's physical inferiority.

We call upon feminist killjoys to resist this patriarchal narrative. Recognizing how men's superiority and women's inferiority is made and remade over time helps us to reject this portrayal and create a new future. It also helps us see how the male/female binary, far from being a simple reflection of reality, is manufactured.

In the killjoy spirit, we understand that sport (as it currently exists) is a patriarchal tool. We believe, too, that this strict policing of gender, assertion of masculinity and upholding of sexual inequalities through sport is, ultimately, a far right, even fascist, project (here drawing on recent work by philosophers Jason Stanley and Kate Manne[5]). This chapter thus deals with women who broke the social contract and beat men in sport, and the consequences that women in sport faced for decades afterwards. *Women's Sport* as a category is no feminist win.

Madge Syers has a great many feminist killjoy sisters. Their stories reveal a pattern of the making of *Women's Sport* as a separate, subordinate category. This pattern has been hidden for far too long. But once it is seen it can never be unseen.

Too delicate for the strenuous game: Jackie Gilbert

Virne Beatrice 'Jackie' Mitchell Gilbert was an American baseball player during the 1920s and '30s. Jackie started playing baseball from a young age and was taught how to pitch by Major League Hall of Famer Dazzy Vance. By the time she was seventeen years old, Jackie was playing for her local women's team, the Engelettes. Later, in 1931, she was signed to the Chattanooga Lookouts by president and owner Joe Engel. Jackie became only the second woman behind Lizzie Arlington to play in a professional men's baseball team (Arlington did so in 1898).

This feat was not surprising since 'America's pastime' had always been played by both men and women. The first organized women's team appeared at Vassar College in 1866 (the Vassar team disbanded in 1978 due to 'parents' concerns over the safety of baseball for their daughters'[6]). By 1907, pitching sensation Alta Weiss joined the Vermilion Independents, a men's semi-professional team, with over 1,200 fans coming to watch her debut. Later, special trains would be commissioned to allow her fans to travel. Women umpires also existed, with sixteen-year-old Amanda Clement becoming the first paid woman umpire, in 1904. She went on to referee fifty games a season. And further, in 1911 Helene Britton became the first woman owner of a Major League Baseball team, the St Louis Cardinals. As such, women were well placed to enter this sport, crossing into the men's game.

It is from this fertile environment that the talented Jackie Mitchell emerged, and in which her signing to the Lookouts was possible. Owner Engel often made use of publicity stunts to draw baseball crowds during the Great Depression, and soon after signing Mitchell he staged an exhibition game against the New York

Yankees. Then seventeen, Jackie was brought in to pitch in the first innings, with both Babe Ruth and Lou Gehrig facing her in quick succession. Ruth swung out with a third strike (reportedly glaring at and verbally abusing the umpire when this happened), and soon after Gehrig did the same. Jackie had just struck out two of the greatest ever baseball players. The crowd cheered for her heartily.

Babe Ruth later seethed: 'I don't know what's going to happen if they begin to let women in baseball. Of course, they will never make good. Why? Because they are too delicate. It would kill them to play ball every day.'[7] The baseball commissioner at the time, Kenesaw Mountain Landis, agreed, and days later voided Mitchell's contract on the grounds that the game was 'too strenuous' for women.[8] Women would later be banned from playing Major League Baseball until 1993. When the All-American Girls Professional Baseball League was formed in 1943, Jackie refused to come out of retirement.

Jackie is a feminist killjoy on two counts. First, she spoilt the dinner of men in baseball by not only participating but, in their eyes, humiliating them. She threatened men's dominance with ultimately devastating consequences both for her professionally and for all women in baseball. This seventeen-year-old girl's feat is often undermined as simply being a stunt, but she maintained until her death that this was not the case. She was simply better, and she exposed men's entitlement. Second, Jackie later recognized the creation of the 'Girls League' for what it was: patronizing. She saw through the benevolent sexism of 'giving girls and women a chance to participate' and recognized the Girls League as a method of control. Separated into a(n inferior) league of their own, girls and women would never be able to threaten men's dominance in baseball again.[9]

Too good, and yet not good enough: Zhang Shan

Years later, women who participated in skeet shooting suffered the same grave consequence as a result of a woman being too good and threatening patriarchal entitlement. Zhang Shan is a Chinese athlete from Nanchong in Sichuan province who started shooting skeet when sixteen years old. In 1992 she was part of the Chinese Olympic Team, participating in the Olympic Skeet Shooting event. Since the inclusion of skeet shooting in the Olympic Games in 1968 it had been a mixed-gender event, meaning that both men and women competed together. And in Barcelona in 1992, as one of only seven women in the sixty-strong field, Zhang not only broke the Olympic record but equalled the world record and won the gold medal. She would be the first and last woman to do so in the event as it stood.

After the 1992 Olympics, the International Shooting Union (ISU, later the ISSF) would ban women from participating with men, in effect banning women from Olympic Skeet Shooting as there was only the one event. With no competitions in which to participate, Zhang was forced to retire from shooting.

The 2000 Sydney Olympics saw the creation of a new women's skeet shooting event. Notably, this event now contained fewer targets (75) than the men's event (125). Zhang came out of retirement, and would compete for the rest of her life, but never reached the lofty heights of 1992 again. Describing her own experience and love of the sport, she said:

If there is an old lady on the skeet range, it must be me. Skeet shooting has been carved into my life. It may reach the last day of my life. Shooting has changed everything

49

for me. I love this sport. I don't think I can leave it in my lifetime.[10]

Zhang's story is another dot in the pattern of the making of *Women's Sport*: a socially subordinate category in which participants are not expected to be as good as in (men's) *Sport* and which receives fewer accolades and support. In this way, sport plays a role in the making and re-making of women's inferior place in society. Far from being an 'opportunity' for women, as it is so often framed, cleaving women off into an inferior form of the sport serves to keep them in their place. Separated into a(n inferior) league of their own, girls and women would never be able to threaten men's dominance in skeet shooting again.[11]

Not physiologically capable: Bobbi Gibb

In 1966 the longest running race that women were allowed to compete in was 1½ miles. The marathon (26.2 miles/42 km) existed but was only open to men. Roberta 'Bobbi' Louise Gibb, an American woman, decided in that year to attempt to enter the Boston Marathon anyway. In response to her application, the race director Will Cloney refused her participation on the grounds that women were 'not physiologically capable of running 26 miles and furthermore, under the rules that governed international sports, they were not allowed to run' (Gibb's own account of the reasons).[12] Bobbi ran anyway, wearing her brother's gear and hiding in the bushes until the race began. She would go on to beat 290 of the event's 415 starters, finishing in a time of 3 hours, 21 minutes and 40 seconds. Race director Cloney afterwards said of Bobbi's run:

Mrs Bingay (Gibb) did not run in yesterday's marathon. There is no such thing as a marathon for a woman. She may have run in a road race, but she did not race in the marathon. I have no idea of this woman running. She was not at any of our checkpoints and none of our checkers saw her. For all I know she could have jumped in at Kenmore Square.[13]

Bobbi would go on to run unofficially again in the following years, alongside a growing number of fellow feminist killjoy women runners, including Kathrine Switzer, Carol Ann Pancko, Elaine Pedersen, Marjorie Fish and Sara Mae Berman. By 1972 the official women's category would be created, which Nina Kuscsik would win. The women's performances between 1966 and 1971 would not be recognized until thirty years later, in 1996. With this recognition, Bobbi would be awarded as the winner of the first three 'Pioneer' *Women's* Boston Marathon races.

Once again, the recognition of a women's category sounds, on first reading, like a positive development for women. Women were being included, and even recognized and lauded retrospectively for their sporting performances. But if we cast a feminist killjoy eye over her story, we can 'bring what has receded into the background to the front, in order to confront it', as Sara Ahmed instructs.[14] Contrary to the easy conclusion that a separate women's category was what these women wanted, Bobbi and her feminist killjoys just wanted to run the Boston Marathon. They wanted to compete in the sport that they loved. Bobbi herself later wrote, 'it was not a men-versus-women confrontation. The men were glad that I was running.'[15] And yet, because the killjoys broke the social contract, and began threatening patriarchal notions about women not being 'physiologically capable' of running the marathon, patriarchy needed to suppress them.

These women threatened the very mechanism for keeping women subordinate and men dominant, physically. If women could run as far as men, and even beat some men in doing so, what else would they realize they were capable of? The denial of women's capability was no longer possible after these performances, but control was. Separating women into a category that would be, as with all *Women's Sport*, under-valued and under-funded by sports organizations became the go-to bait-and-switch. Through the women's category, women could be controlled in various explicit and implicit ways, which ultimately became a hugely effective method for both creating and maintaining the physical gap between men and women. And so, women were sold the benevolent (still sexist) 'win' of a category of their own and were gaslit into being grateful for it. Separated into a(n inferior) category of their own, girls and women would never be able to threaten men's dominance in the marathon again.

Unsuitable for females: *Women's Football* in the UK

This same control manoeuvre would be used in football. In the United Kingdom in the early 1900s, football as a sport in which women participated was thriving. Nettie Honeyball had founded the British Ladies' Football Club in 1894, despite a lack of support from the FA (academic Stefan Mårtensson has, too, suggested that this lack of support was due to the involvement of women threatening masculinity, as we do[16]). Later, during the First World War, as women took up roles that had previously been unthinkable (including heavy-duty ammunitions factory work), football as a pastime emerged as an extremely popular sport for them. By 1920, football played by women, which by now included international games, was regularly drawing crowds of 20,000 spectators. One notable game, at Goodison Park on Boxing Day 1920, drew a crowd of 53,000 fans. Football as a sport that women played, at least in the UK, looked not only promising, but limitless.

But women in England would soon learn that there was indeed a limit. As the First World War drew to a close, men returned home and women were once again relegated to domestic life and feminized professions. At the same time, despite much evidence to the contrary in both factories and football, an old narrative re-emerged: that women were simply not built for strenuous activities. This was, at the time, backed up by scientific and medical evidence. Dame Mary Scharlieb of Harley Street, for example, said of football that it was a 'most unsuitable game, too much for a woman's physical frame'.[17] Many people considered sports like football to be damaging to women's health. As such, by 1921, the FA had banned women from playing on all FA-affiliated grounds and pitches on the basis that 'the game of football is quite unsuitable for females and ought not to be encouraged.' The effect of this was that football for women in England was effectively frozen in its tracks.

Alice Barlow, a player from what had been the extremely successful Dick, Kerr Ladies' Club, later accurately diagnosed the root of the problem, saying, 'we could only put it down to jealousy. We were more popular than the men.'[18] Others have explained that another reason would have been that the FA did not see the money made from women's games, with much of it going to charity. We add to this that women playing football once again threatened masculine dominance.

It was not until 1971, exactly fifty years later, that the FA lifted its ban. It would take another fifty years for the women's game to recover, with 50,000-strong crowds only being regained in the summer of 2022 with the UEFA Women's Euros with which we opened this book. Ironically, many of the current Lionesses have shared their stories of playing on boys' teams while they were growing up, simply because local girls' teams did not exist. Lauren Hemp explicitly credits her success to playing with the boys, saying in a Lionesses programme from 2022 (vs the Netherlands) that 'those games helped shape me as a player because I am quite physical and strong, and I think that stemmed from playing in a boys' team frequently.' From the age of eighteen in England, however, girls can no longer play with boys (a limit raised from sixteen only in the last decade). In the past, this has led to many girls giving up the game since there were no teams available in which they could play.

The stories of women in football show that, far from being too fragile for the game, she is in fact more than capable of the physicality and skill the sport demands. They also show that people, given the chance, will watch women playing football in their droves. It has never been an inherently inferior form of the game, but rather it has actively been made so through the creation of *Women's Football* as a separate, subordinate category. We reject this framing, and prefer to hold on to football that happens to be played by women.

It comes as some surprise to us that, at the time of writing, there is still a strong narrative in some circles that women footballers should be playing on smaller pitches, with smaller balls and smaller goals.[19] The argument goes that, since women are supposedly smaller than men, they should play on smaller terms in order to foster a better version of the game for them. But we reject this call as well. We see this notion as once again serving patriarchy, not women, by keeping women small and under-resourcing them once again (this would effectively lock women out of all existing adult football pitches). Women footballers need investment, high-quality training, professionalization, equal pay and, importantly, equal respect to thrive in the game as it exists. Patronizingly relegating them to a smaller, inferior form of the game would set us back. Women can and do excel on the biggest stages if the conditions are equal. For example, this current generation of world-class women goalkeepers are the first to have access to specialized goalkeeping coaches and are now finally able to prove that they are as good and as skilful as their men counterparts.

Women footballers don't just blow ignorance about women's bodies out of the water, but also show how their effective banning is connected to a woman's place in society and how her social subordination is created, dropped when convenient, recreated when needed and upheld over time.

Save Women's Sports: Lia Thomas

Sport is still being used as a tool to cement women's inferior place in society. Yet this time it is being perpetuated through a new twist on the 'feminist' narrative. In 2022 Lia Catherine Thomas, an American swimmer, became the first openly transgender woman to compete in the NCAA Division 1 National Championship and win an event.

Lia didn't break any records. The record for the event won by Thomas, the 500-yard Freestyle, is held by cisgendered swimmer

Katie Ledecky and is a full 9.18 seconds faster than Lia's time (cis-gendered women are women who were assigned female at birth and their gender identity corresponds). Some of Lia Thomas's times were surpassed by swimmers in 2023 (Lia graduated in 2022, and as such can no longer compete in college events such as the NCAAS). And yet, the outcry over Lia's participation has been outsized. She has been blamed for almost single-handedly orchestrating the death of *Women's Sport*, with many calls in recent years to 'Save Women's Sport' coming from purportedly feminist groups.

Why this outcry? The narrative goes that, as a trans woman, Lia has some sort of sporting advantage over cisgendered women. There has been much speculation about this advantage; however, it isn't borne out by the evidence. Not in Lia's case, and not in the case of any trans woman athlete. Indeed, trans women have competed in women's sport since at least 2004, with women's sport experiencing unprecedented growth since that time. The 'threat' of trans women in women's sport has simply not amounted to the death knell we have been told to expect.

Lia has, through her participation, joined the lineage of the feminist killjoy. Later in this book, we will take up the mantle to explain how her participation *is the feminist path*. We reject the idea that to be feminist we must be anti-trans, and rather hold that the growing anti-trans movements are oppressive and far-right movements. But for now, we want to add another dot to the pattern of the making and remaking of patriarchy in and through sport.

We have provided a number of examples now of instances in which, when women started to undermine men's dominance, patriarchal control emerged. Sport is littered with examples of women being 'too good', threatening men's dominance, and then promptly being relegated to their own category: a category that can be controlled.

In 2022, in response to Lia's participation, World Aquatics introduced regulations for participation in the women's category that effectively resulted in Lia being banned. By 2023 World Aquatics had instituted what they call an 'open category': a segregated category for transgender swimmers. While some laud this as a win for trans athletes, we want to show it for what it is: more patriarchal control. As with the invention of *Women's Sport*, the creation of *Trans Sport* signals an othering and further marginalization: a new category that will be run according to the rules of the (predominantly) men in charge; a new category to be under-invested in, under-supported and under-respected, controlled. Another way to subordinate women.

We hear the narrative that *Trans Sport* is necessary in order to protect *Women's Sport*. To protect women in sport and to give them a chance to win, trans women must be excluded. But this narrative is profoundly paternalistic and keeps women small. Women in sport have shown, time and time again, that, given the resources and support, they can play with the best and hold their own. Women (and all marginalized people, for that matter) don't need patronizing protection: they need equality.

The day when women and people of all marginalized genders can compete against men and win, without the decades-long threat of patriarchal backlash, will be the day we have made progress. Women (all women) who excel at sport are showing just how fragile patriarchy is, and we salute these feminist killjoys for their role in shutting it down, one event, one medal, one sport at a time.

Reframing the narrative: women can and do win

Through the stories of Madge, Jackie, Zhang, women footballers in England, Bobbi and Lia we have shown that the narrative that *Women's Sport* apparently exists as a 'protected category' so that women can win (because according to this account, without it no woman will ever win again) is a concocted one. *Women's Sport* doesn't exist as a category because women don't and can't win overall, but because they do. *Women's Sport* exists as a category because the dominance of men athletes was threatened by women competing, and patriarchy had to reassert control. Women's inclusion wasn't a feminist win, rather it was with benevolent sexism that a woman's category was granted on the terms of those in power. We still see this today. And we still see the ramifications.

In this next section we want to unpack the manufactured narratives about women and sport further by focusing on the myth that women are inherently physically inferior to men. We hold that this myth, far from being 'biological' or 'natural', is one that is created through activities like sport. It is a myth made reality that must be maintained in order to segregate women (and anyone who is not a cis White man) without threatening (White supremacist) masculinity.

i. 'They didn't like to be overtaken by the girls': Margaret Murdock

In 1976 Margaret Murdock was the first woman to compete in air-rifle shooting on the u.s. Olympic Team, for the Montreal Olympic Games. She had previously won two gold medals at the Pan American Games and had set an overall world record for the kneeling rifle shooting event. At the Montreal Olympics, Margaret won the silver medal after tying with Lanny Bassham (the rules did not allow for a tie-break shoot-off, and Bassham was awarded gold after examination of the targets). Bassham, to his credit, pulled Margaret onto the gold podium during the medal presentations.

However, as we've seen previously, Margaret's performance was a threat to men's entitlement. As Heinz Reinkemeier, a shooting coach, later remarked to ESPN in 2021: 'after that the men decided to split shooting up into men and women because they didn't like to be overtaken by the girls.'[20] By 1984, separate events for women were added to the Los Angeles Olympic Games.

Ironically, air-rifle shooting is one of those sports where, even though separated, the rules have remained exactly the same and women have continued to match or outdo the men. Despite this, the existence of separate categories means that the reporting of this is always separate, hiding the fact that women can and do win.

ii. Supposedly artificially boosted by men: Paula Radcliffe

Earlier we discussed the origin of the *Women's* Marathon, and we now turn to a key way in which this category is policed so as not to outshine the (men's) Marathon: the ban on men pace-making for women.

In 2003 Paula Radcliffe, a British athlete, won the London Marathon in a record-breaking time of 2:15:25. But by 2012, Paula's race would be erased from world-record history. Instead, the IAAF (International Association of Athletics Federations, since 2019 World Athletics) relegated her performance to a new 'World Best' category, a separate classification for records set by women in mixed environments (those where men and women run together). Why this decision? The sporting body had decided that running with men was artificially boosting women's performances. Paula always disputed this characterization of mixed marathon environments, stating: 'When I ran that time, I was racing the guys, not getting assistance from them.'[21]

But the IAAF did not see it this way. It argued that women received undue advantage from men pace-making, and in this way justified their decision. Once again, on the surface this argument appears to make sense: women can slipstream or 'draft' off faster men, but men don't have a category of faster people to offer the same – notwithstanding Eliud Kipchoge in 2019 running an unofficial exhibition sub-two-hour marathon using rotating pace-makers and even a car to draft off. As such, the IAAF's ban on men pace-making for women is seemingly one that promotes fairness in the sport. However, if we bring a feminist killjoy criticality to this argument, we can note the many ways in which men in sport have been advantaged through decades of development to which sportswomen simply didn't have access. We can see an argument where women could indeed be faster than men, given half the chance and all of the time and access and resources to get there. Eliud's sub-two-hour marathon may not be an official world record, but it provides men with the role modelling needed to get there, just as Roger Bannister's barrier-breaking four-minute mile did. However, as we have seen across the stories in this chapter, to provide this same aspiration and assistance for women is simply unacceptable to a patriarchal world.

One can't help but notice that Paula Radcliffe's 2003 marathon time was over one hour faster than that of Bobbi Gibb in 1966. In just 37 years women had gone from being believed to be 'not physiologically capable' of running the marathon to coming within seven minutes of the men's winning time (Ethiopia's Gezahegne Abera's 2003 London Marathon time was 2:07:56).

No wonder the patriarchy had to take control, and fast. Women were within glancing distance of challenging men's dominance. And the patriarchal tactic worked. Most road marathons worldwide are run in mixed conditions, and this rule change made access to world-record-eligible marathon races harder for women. After this change in rules, the women's marathon record time stalled, with the men's dropping close to the two-hour mark. In 2021 the IAAF decided to distinguish between the women's world record in a mixed race and the women's world record in a women-only race. When Tigst Assefa broke the record at the 2023 Berlin Marathon, she did so in the mixed race, and ran it more than four minutes faster than the women-only record. Prima facie, this shows that women will perform better when they compete with men than when they are relegated to a category of their own.

iii. Allegedly tactics not talent: Jasmin Paris

Ultra-endurance racing is proving a fascinating and unprecedented shift in how we get to see women in sport: as overall winners.

Jasmin Karina Paris is a British fell runner who, in 2019, won the gruelling 268-mile (431 km) mid-winter Spine Race along the Pennine Way in England and Scotland. She won in 83 hours, 12 minutes and 23 seconds. Jasmin, impressively, didn't *just* win the overall race (men and women), but also beat the previous record by over ten hours (set by Eoin Keith in 2016), *and* did so while expressing milk for her baby during race breaks. This is a remarkable feat for any human.

Sport scientists have tried to explain women's outsized performances in ultra-endurance racing by putting their wins down to tactics, rather than talent. They argue that it is often a woman's skills as a mother, rather than as an athlete, that provide the edge during a race (because women can never simply be great athletes, as men are). There is an argument that women (particularly mothers) are simply naturally more adept at planning, recognizing the importance of nutrition and sleep, and maintaining safety during the course of such a long race. Similarly, we have read arguments that women are more 'emotion-focused' in their coping skills, giving them the edge in ultra-endurance racing. Pain management, too, is often brought up because of women's experiences giving birth. But this narrative essentializes these skills as gendered ones – the domain of (child-bearing) women – and neglects to recognize that these are learned ones that are accessible to all: that this is what makes up an athlete, and that women can be great athletes too. It is curious that this narrative only arises when discussing women who win ultra-endurance races, and not men. When men employ these skills, they are framed as smart 'marginal gains'; when women win, they are 'mothering skills'. Painting tactics as the primary reason why Jasmin won erases her mind-boggling physical feat.

While the Spine Race undeniably requires great planning and support, especially with the added job of expressing milk, the sheer difficulty of this race also requires excellent physical abilities. And, as Jasmin once again shows, women can and do win. We feel that this belittling of her physicality by putting her win down to tactics is once again symptomatic of patriarchal mechanisms of control: women can't simply be great at sport, it must always be something else. Attributing success to traditionally feminine traits as a way of explaining her win simultaneously downplays her physical feat and reinforces her role as a mother in a patriarchal society. A woman can never simply be a brilliant athlete.

Ultra-endurance racing is fast becoming a fascinating space that is breaking down gendered barriers. The past ten years have seen unprecedented growth in women participating in these demanding sports, and with that has come remarkable break-throughs into top ten rankings, and outright wins. Unable to comprehend that women can simply be great athletes in ultra-endurance racing (and, we might add, in all sports), a lot of focus has been on trying to find social and physiological reasons that will explain what our biased minds register as anomalies. The feminist killjoy, however, is able to recognize this bias and interrogate it; women can and do win just because they are excellent athletes.

iv. We can't compare: Maya Gabeira

In 2020 Brazilian surfer Maya Gabeira potentially set a new world record for big wave surfing. Her big wave surf on 11 February in Nazaré, Portugal, was hailed by many as the biggest wave surfed by anyone that year. But as journalist Maggie Mertens documented for *The Atlantic*:

> Gabeira's historic win was light on fanfare, with the news hampered by an uncharacteristically long delay (about four weeks after the men's announcement), and also because her achievement was subject to a brand-new and completely different set of measuring criteria than was required for the men's waves.[22]

Up until this point, big wave surfing had always been judged on a fairly imprecise and subjective basis. While Kai Lenny's 70-foot (21⅓ m) men's winning wave was announced immediately, it was decided that further scientific scrutiny was needed for

Maya's wave, and a sixteen-page report was produced. The World Surf League (WSL) justified this as necessary due to the closeness of the top two women's waves that year.

Of this decision, Mertens writes:

> on its face, further review of the women's competition would seem to be a good thing, to make this award more data-driven in a year of a tight race and a new potential world record. But doing so now with just the women's wave, and at the last minute of judging, has raised questions.[23]

These questions are ones of gender bias. Big wave surfing, as sociologist Holly Thorpe explained to Mertens, is 'that kind of last bastion of surfing that is still very male-dominated, and it reinforces a particular type of masculinity. So when [women] challenge that, they're really challenging all of those ideas.'[24]

In the end, Maya's world record wave was confirmed at 73.5 feet (22.4 m), with Justine Dupont's just a couple of feet smaller. Notably, however, both women surfed bigger waves than the men's winner. The decision to apply extra scrutiny to the women's achievements, and in doing so delaying the announcement of their incredible wave heights by a month, meant that a further achievement was downplayed: the fact that two women had surfed bigger waves than any man that year. Maya had won the competition outright. The WSL went to great lengths to avoid making this the story, however. They repeatedly emphasized that the men's and women's competitions were judged separately (and differently, for the first time that year), and continually highlighted that Maya had won the *women's division*. It is not difficult to suspect that the extra scrutiny and delay in announcing her wave height created an opportunity for the WSL to control the narrative, minimizing the opportunity for recognition of Maya's outright win. This is a common tactic.

Maya's (and Justine's) performance shows, once again, that a woman can and does beat men. And yet, when she does, she unlocks deep fears about women's power. The methods may be indirect and draped in scientism, but the patriarchal control continues.

v. Too good to be a woman: Caster Semenya

Mokgadi Caster Semenya is a South African middle-distance runner born in 1991. She has won gold medals in the women's 800-metre event at the 2009, 2011 and 2017 World Championships, and the 2012 and 2016 Olympic Games.

Ever since her 2009 senior debut, Caster has been under immense public and sporting-body scrutiny, not because her performances were wildly outside the range of the women's event (notably, Caster has never held a world record), but because she didn't look like what society expects a woman athlete to look like. Caster is a Black woman who is lean and muscular. Unlike her competitors in athletics who are often feminine presenting, she is a masculine-presenting woman. This is even more obvious next to her Global North White women competitors, who are often petite, feminine, blonde women. Caster does not conform to White, Western ideals of femininity and this has brought her an inordinate amount of unfair scrutiny (which we detail in the next chapter), particularly given the fact that she has never come under doping suspicion and that her performances are not outside the realm of expectation for the women's event.

Caster's experience presents a new, insidious narrative that unmistakeably mirrors the history of *Women's Sport* that we have discussed so far. We hear that some women are supposedly 'too good' at sport, and thus must be separated into their own category in order to give 'real' women the opportunity to win. Caster is a woman with a sex variation: she is sometimes described as an intersex woman, though this term is now outdated and considered stigmatizing. Rather than recognizing these women as women, patriarchy has leapt at the opportunity to further embed hierarchy and control. The narrative has become that cisgendered women need to be 'protected' from women with sex variations (and even more recently, trans women) in order to give them a fair chance of winning. While this argument, once again, appears at face value to be a worthy one, the feminist killjoy knows to look deeper.

The regulation of women with sex variations and trans women in *Women's Sport* is a method of controlling *all* women in sport. The story goes that cisgendered women will never be able to beat a woman with sex variations or a trans woman (despite evidence to the contrary). We are sold fears that we need to 'save women's sports'. However, if we look closely, we can diagnose the root of these fears as being more about the threat such women pose to men's dominance in sport. Despite the fact that these women are not routinely taking (cis) women's or men's medals, our biases read them as being too good to be women.

Women with sex variations and trans women's inclusion is now once again on the terms of those in power. These women are subject to medical scrutiny and regulation (including unnecessary surgical and medical intervention) in order to be 'allowed' to participate in the women's category. Further, we are once again seeing a call for separation into a new category. This is the latest iteration in a long history of regulating women who are somehow supposedly *too good.*

Women like Caster are often positioned as being a threat to women's sport, but the feminist killjoy recognizes the bait-and-switch. Women with sex variations don't and have never threatened women's sport (there has been no anomalous dominance by these women); rather, they threaten patriarchy by providing a different image of who a woman can be. Women in sport have most often had the added burden of performing femininity so as not to threaten patriarchy, yet here is a woman who refuses to play that game. She is simply herself, and an excellent athlete for that matter. And in doing so, she shows all women a new path forward, one that can in the future threaten the carefully curated image of men's dominance and women's subordinance. Gender expansiveness is the biggest threat to patriarchy, and this is why these women are subject to the harshest of its controls.

We will end by saying that it is no coincidence that primarily Black and Brown women from the Global South, who do not conform to Western, White ideals of femininity, are at the centre of calls for regulation. However, what these women threaten is not other women but rather patriarchal White supremacy; the backlash is about control. Control of *all* women. Patriarchy simultaneously threatens women when they are too good, and tells them they'll never be good enough.

Sport has always been political for women. In this chapter we have flipped the script on deeply embedded cultural narratives and tropes about women's bodies (including the myth of women being 'the weaker sex'): narratives that patriarchy enables and that enable patriarchy. We have shown how widespread problematic ignorance about women's bodies is created and upheld through sport, and its connection to the cementing of women's inferior place in society. We have shown that, far from being a feminist win, the category of *Women's Sport* is a method for maintaining subordination and control: an insurance policy to ensure that women will never beat men. We take a feminist killjoy look at the creation of *Women's Sport* and the work it continues to do today, including upholding a continued and active contemporary backlash against equal rights and opportunities for women. Rather than truly providing equality, the division into *Sport* and *Women's Sport* is a patriarchal tool to maintain men's superiority and women's subordinance. We hold that feminism should prioritize sport and physicality as a feminist issue, and thereby position sports feminism and *Feminist Sport* as being about far more than sport alone.

3

Policing Women's Sport

What is a woman? This seemingly straightforward question has fast become the biggest 'issue' of *Women's Sport*.[1] Even outside of sport, it is positioned as an urgent and unavoidable question, with politicians and others in positions of authority expected to present a simple, single-sentence answer. Sport is proving to be a particular focus of this discussion, however, where it gets hastily connected with matters of fairness and safety. We repeatedly hear fears of male 'imposters' in women's sport, of women never being able to win again because of them, and even of women's sport disappearing altogether. As a result, anxieties about who is and isn't allowed to participate and compete in the women's category are increasingly leading to renewed calls for sex verification in sport. As we will make clear in this chapter, however, much of this discussion is spurious and, indeed, disingenuous. Furthermore, the definition of a woman is an almost entirely manufactured 'issue' or 'debate' both inside and outside of sport. We will tell the story of 'sex verification', revealing a history in which women's bodies have been policed in several ever-changing and intrusive ways as a precondition of their participation in sport. This has imposed an additional burden on women that has never been asked of men, acting as a further barrier to women's inclusion.

Verifying whether someone is a woman for the purposes of sport is not a new phenomenon. So-called 'sex verification' (also known as 'gender verification' or 'sex testing' – we see these terms as interchangeable for the purposes of this context) has been around since at least the 1940s. With the growing participation of women in sport in the early 1900s, as we saw in Chapter Two, patriarchal notions about women's weakness and fragility were being challenged. Sportswomen were showing that far from being an 'unsuitable' activity for women, sport was a pathway to liberation. These women not only shattered absurd notions about not being capable of physical pursuits, but unlocked new capabilities that went far beyond sport alone. Women were learning that they too could be strong and powerful; their bodies (and minds) were not limiting factors as they'd always been told, but rather were capable of extraordinary things. Furthermore, they were revealing that, far from being 'the weaker sex', women can and did outcompete men in sport and beyond. Through sport, women had discovered that the supposed gulf between men and women was not as large as they had once imagined and, indeed, that perhaps the 'two sexes' had more similarities than differences. Maybe the very idea of 'two sexes' was itself a myth. These athletes had unlocked a gateway to equality that was about far more than just sport.

But with the discovery of this gateway came the arrival of immense gatekeeping. Sportswomen provided all women with the key to understanding that they are fully human too. Our species isn't simply *man* or *mankind*. This represented an existential threat to the status quo. Chapter Two explained the first mechanism of patriarchal gatekeeping that kicked in: the creation of the women's category (the invention of *Women's Sport*). In this chapter, we present a second: the policing of women's bodies (who gets to be a 'real' woman).

Woman's incompatibility with being an athlete

In the process of writing this book, Sheree undertook a writing retreat at a residential library, Gladstone's Library, in North Wales. She chose a desk to work at for the duration of her time there on the basis that it was on the second floor with a beautiful view. As the week went on, she realized that she had chosen a desk coincidentally right next to the section on the Ministry of Women. Books with titles such as *When Women Become Priests, Presiding Like a Woman, Feminine in the Church* and *Crossing the Boundary* became her writing companions. On the last day of her retreat, Sheree became particularly intrigued by an 1891 book by a certain Ernest Mason entitled *Womanhood in the God-Man*. Opening it up, she learned about the 'Characteristics of Womanhood':

> The female form, although it may possess a great strength and energy, yet has a beautiful delicacy of construction. Its whole appearance is not that of strength, but of beauty, refinement, and tenderness. The outlines of it are soft, yielding, and flexible. The frame is like a delicate mechanism – not the mechanism of a locomotive, but of a loom or watch. The nerves are of a sensitive fibre; the skin is of the finest texture; the limbs in general have a quickness of movement, and the hands a rich softness in their touch. The human frame of a woman is capable of boundless susceptibility. Its readiness to feel is wonderful . . . How tender is the delicacy of her nature;

like a sensitive plant, she will retire into the shadow, and dwell there, and from secret places send forth an odour of sweetness, as a violet sheltered in the shade. Her existence is an influence more than a personality. Perhaps it is here that we touch on one of the fairest virtues of womanhood, that of modesty. It is its attraction; it is its power; it is its beauty. The lily's glory is not in its garments of white, nor in the sweetness of its fragrance, but in its humility; for it loves to shelter its snowy form of grace beneath the wide leaves, and find seclusion among the broken bracken of the gloomy wood. This delicacy of nature shows itself throughout in her appearance, her manners, her refinement of sentiment, her gentleness of speech – shrinking from notoriety and the public gaze, aversion to the course, abhorrence of all that is impure, either in action or in principle . . . so delicate is her mechanism . . . the weakness of woman is found in her infirmity.[2]

Chloe Kelly's flagrant flaunting of her sports bra would clearly not please Mr Mason. There was nothing modest about her behaviour at all. Further, Sheree learned from Mr Mason about the frame of a woman:

The whole frame of woman is of a more delicate construction; the outline of the figure is more graceful, more flowing; the nervous system is more subtle and sensitive. The limbs are weaker and less robust; there is a greater refinement of bearing – a greater softness in the general movement; the skin is of a much finer texture . . . It is apparent that there is less muscular strength; her chest is less capacious; the bones less projecting; the muscles softer, more smoothly blended one into the other; the shoulders are more narrow and rounded; the hair smooth and of a more silken appearance; the brain is smaller and weighs less than that of a man by about five ounces . . . we shall find a corresponding deficiency in mental ability and vigour.[3]

Given this prevailing view of what women *are*, as *Women's Sport* gained popularity in the early to mid-twentieth century, and women's sporting prowess began to take hold, a new question emerged: *were these even women?* Femininity defined womanhood. Womanhood is soft, nurturing and fragile. A woman's main purpose in life is childbearing. She is passive and delicate. These qualities are incompatible with being an athlete. If sport is defined as the voluntary overcoming of unnecessary obstacles, following philosopher Bernard Suits in *The Grasshopper* (2005), then woman simply does not have the mettle.[4] As Mason says:

The inferiority of will power is manifest in the different way in which a woman treats obstacles from the way in which a man treats the same. In woman there is not found that dogged perseverance, the stern determination to overcome difficulties, that is found in man . . . In woman, instead of these energetic ploddings, there is a tendency to submit to rather than surmount the obstacles of life.[5]

Sport demands masculinity. And masculinity is manhood.

In giving a general review of the difference between men and women, we might say that men are brave, audacious, enterprising, prosaic, calculating, pertinacious, authoritative, grave, immovable, exacting, severe, robust, liberal in public, despotic in private, independent, self-seeking; whereas women are gentle, pretty, timid, resigned, poetical, sentimental, flighty, frivolous, nervous, tender, pious, chaste, modest, demure, fond of retirement, self-sacrificing, tearful.[6]

Strength, competitiveness, ruthlessness, vigour: qualities incompatible with being a woman. Ergo, women simply could not be athletes. And in case anyone thinks, or hopes, that Mason's was a sole and eccentric voice of the nineteenth century, we could also draw attention to American Frederick Hollick's *The Diseases of Woman: Their Causes and Cure Familiarly Explained* (1847), particularly the chapter on hysteria (a common medical diagnosis of the era describing an affliction solely of women, since the uterus is understood, at this time, to be their organ of control instead of the brain). Also consider Donald Walker's *Exercises for Ladies* (1836), which are naturally a gentler set of exercises than those recommended in his companion volume *Manly Exercises*! Writing towards the end of the Victorian era, Mason wasn't writing anything he thought would be particularly controversial but articulating a view commonly held. As scientist Lucy Cooke explains, this view of the passivity of women gained the ultimate seal of approval in the biological sciences in Charles Darwin's *The Descent of Man, and Selection in Relation to Sex* (1871).[7]

As such, doctors and sports authorities became increasingly alarmed by women competing in sport. Worries about women's reproductive capacity being harmed were at the forefront of their concerns. Anxieties about women becoming 'manly' and unattractive to men became commonplace. As sportswomen got stronger and more athletic, they were increasingly castigated for their rejection of femininity and embracing of masculinity. This expansive societal shift of what a woman could be became an existential threat to a patriarchal society. If women were not becoming 'real' women (passive and subordinate) but rather more like men (active and dominant), who would be left to enact women's roles in society? A crisis seemed to be looming. Mason continues:

> What a revolting thing it is for anyone to behold an unwomanly woman – one who has forgotten all that gives her beauty and her glory; she who, for the sake of bravado or other low motive, puts on the qualities of the opposite sex, puts off her womanliness. They are not a part of her nature. She has not grown into them; she has affected them. And affectation is vulgarity. It is disgusting in any person to ape qualities he does not possess. I do not say imitation, which is different from apeing. But when it comes to woman apeing the characteristics of man it becomes a disdainful sight. As soon as this is done she has lost her power and influence. As a woman she was invulnerable. Now, she is assailable from every point. Her glory has departed with her womanhood.[8]

The creation of the women's category had only partly managed to achieve its goal of containing feminist killjoy women. As we discussed in Chapter Two, the making of *Women's Sport* had been the response to women showing not only that they could compete with men, but that they could challenge their dominance. But here, even in a category of their own (which was often a lesser version of the original, as we saw with skeet shooting in Chapter Two), women were doing just that. This time, however, they weren't proving a challenge simply to men's physicality, but to their very roles in society.

Sports authorities' next move became clear: they had to restrict *Women's Sport* to 'true' women. If sport was restricted only to 'real' women, surely this growing problem of 'mannish' women (Unwomen? Non-women?) who were taking up too much space could be contained. Of course, people have always existed on a spectrum of masculine to feminine, with both of the poles, and more, being accessible to all. There have always been masculine women and feminine men, as well as trans, intersex, non-binary, genderfluid and gender expansive people (though we may not always have recognized them and may have used different words in the past). Rather than simply being a reflection of two distinct human classes (male and female), sport (and other social domains) creates them.

In the twentieth century, and to this day, as we'll see, sport leaned firmly on its role in strictly upholding the two classes of people Mason describes: men and women. Even though (in parts of the world, at least, such as with the campaign of suffragettes in Great Britain) women during this time had fought for and won the right to be recognized as equal human beings rather than a sex class that could be subordinated, sport was a domain that continued to do the work of rigidly upholding the Christo-patriarchal divisions between men and women. Because women in sport were beginning to blur the lines between male and female, and even go beyond them, sporting authorities saw it as their duty to reassert control: to defend 'civilized' society itself (which, as we'll discuss, was always a White supremacist project). Woman had benevolently been 'given' a class of her own in *Women's Sport*, but because she had taken a mile when she'd only been given an inch – by becoming more athlete than woman – patriarchy clamped down. The solution? Sex verification.

Nude parades

The first iteration of 'sex verification' (or, deciding who is a woman and who is not) emerged in the 1940s. Scholar Mireia Garcés de Marcilla Musté, who has traced the origins of sex verification testing to 1946 when national sporting bodies began utilizing the practice, writes:

> The gradual acceptance of women in sports competitions in the early twentieth century was followed by increasing fears about female athletes not being 'true' women. Helen Stephens, who won the gold medal for the 100 meter race in Berlin 1936, was accused of being a man by her competitors and the 'height, musculature and masculine features' of the silver medallist in the same event, Stella Walasiewczowna, also prompted questions about her womanhood.[9]

Between 1946 and 1966, according to Garcés de Marcilla Musté, the onus was on national sporting federations to 'validate' the womanhood of their athletes in the women's category. Where this was done, most often it would have been achieved through the athlete's physician providing some sort of 'femininity certificate'. In 1966, spurred on by often spurious, racist fears of cheating through the supposed use of male impostors in women's sport by Eastern Bloc countries, the IOC (International Olympic Committee) instituted gynaecological inspections and/or visual inspections to ensure that all athletes in the women's category had 'female genitalia'. In reality, these became subjective and crude 'nude parades' in which athletes had to show their genitalia to a panel which would deem them a woman or not.

Note that there were no corresponding nude parades for men. They did not have to show their genitals in order to prove themselves, or as a condition of competing. Men would rightly consider it not only unnecessary but improper and outrageous if they were obligated to do so. Men are simply the default humans or athletes. For any number of reasons, men might not want to expose their genitals to anyone and would most likely consider doing so irrelevant to their participation in sport. Men and women are in very different situations.

Chromosome testing

Because these nude parades fast garnered a reputation for being indecent and humiliating, the IOC opted instead for a different approach: laboratory testing through chromosomal scrutiny (also known as the Barr body test), which they considered 'more dignified', entailing 'minimal physical and psychological disturbance'.[10] Chromosomal testing was mandated for all athletes competing in the women's category in IAAF and IOC events until 1992 (Princess Anne of the UK, interestingly, was the only woman ever exempted when she competed at the 1976 Montreal Olympic Games).

Chromosomal testing is today often billed as a simple cheek swab that is performed only once, and so supposedly is a quick, easy and harm-free approach. The test is used to determine whether a person has XX or XY chromosomes. For the IOC, a confirmation of XX chromosomes determined eligibility for the women's category (with XY determining ineligibility). There was no comparable testing required for athletes in the men's category. While the vast majority of athletes in the women's category surely did indeed experience this as a quick and simple test that determined their eligibility, the IOC experienced flaws in, and pushback against, its 'more dignified' approach. In 2000 a commentary published in the *Journal of the American Medical Association* (*JAMA*) stated:

> In reality, gender verification tests are difficult, expensive, and potentially inaccurate ... these tests fail to exclude all potential impostors, are discriminatory against women with disorders of sexual development, and may have shattering consequences for athletes who 'fail' a test.[11]

This is because chromosomal tests look for an inactive X chromosome. For people with XX chromosomes, the second X remains inactive (in tests it appears as a small mark attached to the cell membrane, called the Barr body, rather than a full active chromosome). For those with XY chromosomes, this Barr body is absent.

However, human bodies are not that simple. Women with Turner syndrome, for example, only have one X chromosome and as such would 'fail' the test. So too would women who have X and Y chromosomes. Ironically, men with Klinefelter syndrome (meaning they have two X chromosomes and one Y chromosome) would pass the test as a woman because of their extra X chromosome. Indeed, there are a number of variations of sex development that exist in humans, and as such the blunt tool that is chromosomal testing can get it 'wrong'. Assuming that all women have XX chromosomes and all men have XY chromosomes is far too simplistic and does not match up to the messy reality of human biology. This complication matters for sports bodies like the IOC in their attempt to neatly separate the categories into women and men according to XX and XY chromosomes. While these syndromes are not common, they show that being a man or woman cannot be reduced simply to chromosome type: it is possible to be a woman, or a man, without the typical chromosomes usually found with that gender. So being a man or woman must be something more. As a corollary, of course, it means that sex testing based on chromosomes alone is fallible.

Most of us don't know our exact chromosomal arrangement. For most intents and purposes, this information is meaningless in our everyday lives (unless coupled with a medical condition that we may need treatment for – but, even so, doctors rarely need to know chromosomal arrangement to be able to treat patients). For athletes who were born girls and grew up to be women, finding out that they had 'failed' this test because they did not have a specific chromosomal arrangement, and thus were not considered women at all for the purposes of sport, was understandably devastating. Famously this is what happened to South African athlete Caster Semenya, talked about in Chapter Two and whose story we will discuss further later.

So it was that the IOC abandoned chromosomal sex testing in 1992 for being too unreliable, recognizing that it was, after all, neither dignified nor accurate for all women. Indeed, they went as far as to recognize that this test 'didn't work, was a public relations nightmare and female athletes objected'.[12] At this time, the IOC switched briefly to using a Polymerase Chain Reaction (PCR) test that searched for 'male-related genetic material' in DNA samples. However, this approach too was subject to much of the same criticism. By 1999 the IOC abolished the practice of this type of sex testing altogether.

This testing approach failed because the IAAF and IOC had taken the flawed idea that athleticism resides in masculinity (which was what the initial nude parades were somehow meant to assess) and had draped it in scientism. Underpinning chromosomal and PCR testing was the idea that, somehow, the Y chromosome contained the very essence of masculinity and manhood (and thus sporting prowess). If a woman did not have two X chromosomes, then she must have an X and a Y, the story went. And if this was the case then she wasn't a woman at all. This is a myth that still lives on today.

Gender verification

It is no surprise that it was the IAAF, having long been at the fore-front of sex testing, who pioneered the methods that went on to be used in the early twenty-first century. In 2006 the organization developed its new Policy on Gender Verification, which aimed to go beyond laboratory testing alone. The policy was also now administered on a 'test if you suspect' basis, rather than being mandated for all. It involved a multitude of medical screens and tests, including by gynaecologists, endocrinologists, internal medicine specialists and psychologists.

It was hoped that this new policy approach would be more acceptable to woman athletes. The intention was that this would lessen the impact on athletes by only verifying those athletes who came under suspicion of not being a woman. But this failed to recognize the harm and humiliation that suspicion itself would cause. Now any woman athlete who failed to live up to some unspoken, arbitrary view of how a woman 'should' look came under scrutiny. Furthermore, anyone could report an athlete if they had doubts about her womanhood, and this developed into a culture of suspicion, judgement and mistrust. Athletes in the women's category were soon under more bodily scrutiny than ever before; competitors, opposing teams, officials and even the media became the 'police' working on behalf of the IAAF.

It was in this context that Indian athlete Santhi Soundarajan attempted suicide after experiencing the deep shame and humiliation of garnering suspicion, being made to undergo gender verification procedures, 'failing' those tests and then being stripped of her 2006 Asian Games silver medal. Santhi had grown up in an impoverished, rural area of India and sport had liberated her, giving her opportunities she could previously only have dreamed of. But now this had all been taken from her because the IAAF deemed that she wasn't a 'real woman'. But Santhi is a woman, and a cisgendered woman at that (she was assigned female at birth, and this corresponds with her gender identity). She has lived her whole life as a girl and then woman, and yet this sports organization had suddenly deemed her not a woman. Santhi was devastated. At the very least, this can put sporting authorities in a morally dubious position. Worse, it could be understood as a very deep violation of another human being.

What support would they offer for someone whose whole identity they had overturned?

She later leaned back into her love of sport, using a cash reparation of 1.5 million rupees (that she was awarded by Tamil Nadu Chief Minister Karunanidhi for her 2006 Asian Games performance, despite being stripped of her medal by the IAAF) to sponsor athletes at her sports academy in Pudukkottai, India. But her own sporting career was over.

In 2009 South African middle-distance runner Mokgadi Caster Semenya would also (as touched on in Chapter Two) come under suspicion for not being woman enough by IAAF standards. The IAAF would justify its decision to mandate that Caster undergo gender verification testing by essentially saying that she was 'too good' to be a woman athlete. It is no coincidence that Caster also, as a Black woman from South Africa, looked nothing like the very feminine White blonde women from Europe. Her muscular body and short hair read as masculine to the European eyes that scrutinized her. Caster indeed dared to be good at her sport, though she never actually even came close to breaking a world record. Nevertheless, the IAAF said it was 'obliged to investigate' whether Caster was, in fact, a 'real' woman.

Caster underwent gender verification scrutiny under a cloud of suspicion and, it would later be determined, without full consent. She was a young athlete, also from an impoverished, rural area in South Africa, whose budding sporting career was now at the mercy of the medical staff working on behalf of the IAAF. Echoing Santhi's story exactly, Caster is a woman – a cisgendered woman who has lived her whole life as a girl and then woman – and yet this sports organization was putting her under the microscope because she didn't conform to what they deemed a woman 'should' look like and 'should' achieve. Speaking in an HBO interview in 2022, Caster would say of this experience: 'They thought I had a dick, probably . . . I told them: "It's fine. I'm a female, I don't care. If you want to see I'm a woman, I will show you my vagina. All right?"'[13]

This quotation shows up the deep underlying assumptions at play here: the penis as the wellspring of sporting (and other) excellence. This notion is a cornerstone of patriarchy. An excellent athlete had to be a man, because this was incompatible with being a woman. Further, Caster was not 'feminine' enough, and as such this only confirmed suspicions that she was not a 'real' woman.

Caster would be allowed to return to competition in 2010 after being cleared to run under the existing protocols. In 2011, however, the IAAF would change course radically in a move away from this 'gender verification' procedure (which, as we'll discuss later, is subjective and open to misinterpretation) and towards testosterone as a proxy for manhood.

Mirroring the reasons for the earlier shift away from chromosome and PCR testing towards gender verification screening, the IAAF gender verification approach had also been an implementation and public relations disaster. Accusations of systemic and scientific racism were at the forefront of this, given that Black and Brown athletes from the Global South were much more likely to come under suspicion for not conforming to White, Western standards of femininity. In the context of narratives that women supposedly need a 'protected category', we can also now begin to see how, as Dr Ruth Pearce and colleagues explain, 'safety' (and we would add 'fairness') becomes subservient to the protectionist politics around (cisgendered) women's bodies, where what is really protected is the ideal of White female vulnerability.[14] The

IAAF must have recognized the immense pressure that the body had put itself under to rectify the blatant subjectivity of its gender verification regulations. The association duly turned again to what it could sell as a more objective, 'scientific' approach: testosterone testing and limits.

Testosterone testing

The American academics Rebecca Jordan-Young, a feminist scientist, and anthropologist and bioethicist Katrina Karkazis explain, in the 2019 book *Testosterone: An Unauthorized Biography*, the myths by which testosterone, over the course of the 2000s and 2010s, came to represent the new essence of masculinity, manhood and thus sporting prowess. Sporting organizations, now firmly entrenched behind the idea that the women's category needed to be policed, bought into this trend, turning to testosterone as their new holy grail.

Testosterone itself is the stuff of deep, enduring folklore. The most potent of beliefs about the molecule is that testosterone is the very essence of masculinity. Seen to be residing in the testes and most often associated with male puberty, we understand testosterone as central to 'masculine' traits such as sex drive, body hair and a deep voice. Correspondingly, we are under the strong impression that strength, competitiveness, ruthlessness and vigour (the athletic traits that we introduced above) all stem almost exclusively from testosterone. Testosterone is understood as being what makes a man. Indeed, testosterone is man. And because a woman doesn't have testes (or a penis, for that matter), she simply does not have access to this fountainhead of masculinity and its associated traits. Unless there is something wrong with her, of course. As we have already seen, the traits associated with testosterone/manhood/sporting prowess (for these are one and the same) in a patriarchal world are incompatible with being a woman. So a woman who has testosterone/masculinity/sporting prowess simply cannot be a woman at all.

It was with these underpinning assumptions (perhaps not explicitly, but most definitely implicitly) that the IAAF in 2011 introduced testosterone testing and limits for women athletes. The organization decided arbitrarily on a limit of 10 nanomoles of endogenous testosterone (made within the body, as opposed to exogenous, which would be doping) per litre of blood for women. If women athletes were found to be above this threshold, they would have to undergo further androgen sensitivity testing, since androgen sensitivity determines whether their bodies can actually use that testosterone. Just because someone has high testosterone levels doesn't mean that they always have the corresponding receptors that allow them to make use of that testosterone. But if a woman athlete was determined to have high testosterone levels *and* androgen sensitivity, she would be ineligible for IAAF competitions. Eligibility could, however, be regained by taking medication to reduce her natural testosterone levels, or through surgery.

Why is the eligibility rule stated in terms of a *limit* on testosterone? It has to be because women have testosterone too: women naturally make testosterone and need it for healthy functioning. As Karkazis explains, 'The number one misconception is that it's a male sex hormone.'[15] On the contrary, testosterone is a hormone that every human needs to function. Testosterone levels also vary widely in men and women, fluctuate according to cycles, and furthermore are concentrated differently and work differently in different areas of the body. As such, we can understand blood testosterone-level testing to be a flawed and meaningless proxy *for anything*, much less womanhood and manhood.

And yet, because our cultural mythology about testosterone as the 'male sex hormone', and the very essence of manhood, is so strong, sporting authorities were blinded by their own biases about the molecule and the meaning they ascribed to it in the development of testosterone-level policies. They had decided that a woman with too much testosterone can't really be a 'true' woman (especially if she didn't conform to White, Western standards of femininity) and had to be brought into line. Of course, they didn't explicitly frame it in this way, and they likely didn't even recognize that their underpinning logic was based on these biases and prejudices. Rather, their justification was that any woman who has too much of the hormone must have some sort of medical condition that gives her an unfair advantage over other women (a medical condition that made her more man-like than woman-like). She was too much man and not enough woman, and this imbalance had to be rectified before she would be allowed to compete in the women's category again. This approach would later be used to police trans women too. Note again, however, that no such rule has ever been imposed on those competing in the men's category. Men are allowed to participate irrespective of their level of endogenous testosterone and no one says that it is unfair if one athlete has a far higher level than his opponents. Why are men treated differently here? Perhaps victory is seen as the just reward for being naturally 'more manly' than one's rivals.

Two women who were deemed 'too manly' through this policy were Indian sprinter Dutee Chand and Caster Semenya.

Both women were determined by the IAAF, under the new policy, to be *hyperandrogenous,* meaning that they had high levels of natural testosterone. As such, both women were banned from competing until they brought down their natural testosterone levels to within the acceptable 'female range' set by the IAAF, on the grounds that this testosterone provided them with an unfair advantage. It is very important to note here that endogenous testosterone (which, to repeat, occurs naturally in the body) works very differently from exogenous testosterone (testosterone added to the body, for example via doping). It is too easy to conflate the two, and we believe that the IAAF has used this to its advantage: we can so easily assume that women with high endogenous testosterone levels have the same advantages that athletes who are doping with testosterone have.

In reality, the science of this issue is quite clear. From a scientific and medical standpoint, we know that testosterone is not the only, or even primary, indicator of sporting performance. Indeed, there are many other factors at play, including training, funding and access to resources, in the development of a winning athlete. Why do we not make a fairness argument so vociferously when it comes to these other – far more significant – determinants of sporting success? Why do we not try to police these inequalities?

Caster complied reluctantly, under extreme duress, and took medication to lower her natural testosterone levels in order to continue competing. Dutee, however, followed a different path. In 2015 she took the IAAF to the Court of Arbitration for Sport (CAS, an appeals tribunal set up by sporting bodies) and won her case on the grounds that there was a lack of evidence that naturally occurring testosterone provides women with an unfair advantage. CAS suspended the testosterone regulations but still gave the IAAF two years to come up with the evidence to support the claim at the centre of their policy. Only then would the policy be implemented.

By 2018, the IAAF had come up with the evidence needed to reinstate its policy. While IAAF researchers were unable to show that all women with high levels of natural testosterone had a competitive advantage, they had data to show that *some* women with high testosterone had an advantage in *some* events. As such, the scope of their policy had to be much narrower; but they were happy to proceed on this basis.

The updated 2018 IAAF policy thus applied only to eight events (those between 400 metres and 1 mile) and only to those athletes in the women's category who had what they deemed a difference of sex development (now defined by the IAAF as a woman with a blood testosterone level of 5 nanomoles per litre and who is androgen sensitive). It was only under these specific circumstances that the IAAF could show that an unfair advantage may exist, making for a complicated policy that had very little prima facie validity. This version of the policy only succeeded in raising more questions. How could women with high natural testosterone levels have advantages only in these specific eight events? What if those same women switched to different events? And why 5 nmol/l (nanomoles per litre) of blood this time, as opposed to the 10 previously? The scientific study conducted by IAAF researchers to support their claim for this new, narrow policy has subsequently been shown to be deeply flawed. Indeed, the authors have since been forced to acknowledge major errors in the data used for the research.[16] Further, new research by sociologist Anna Posbergh, engaging with experts involved in the process of developing protective policies (namely female eligibility policies), has revealed that even these experts understand that the science is flawed.[17]

In non-athletes, endogenous testosterone ranges are normally between 0.4 and 2.0 nmol/l in girls and women. In elite women athletes, however, the testosterone range has been shown to be normally between 0.4 and 7.7 nmol/l; but some women can and do have much higher levels than that, which can also overlap with men's normal ranges. So an arbitrary 5 nmol/l limit for women could have the effect of capturing and regulating a much larger group of female athletes than intended (including women with polycystic ovary syndrome, who naturally have high levels of testosterone).

Despite these flaws, the IAAF forged onwards with implementing the 2018 policy. While some women athletes who fell foul of this policy would go on to reduce their testosterone levels (either through medication or surgery, and not always with fully informed consent), others switched to events not covered by the policy. This time, it was Semenya who took the IAAF to the CAS. In many ways, it seemed that the IAAF was targeting her specifically, as all her events were mysteriously covered by this policy. Furthermore, the medication that she had been forced to take to lower her natural testosterone levels and continue competing made her feel constantly nauseous.

The CAS ultimately sided with the IAAF this time and rejected Caster's challenge. The IAAF had provided the evidence CAS had demanded, no matter how flawed that evidence would later be shown to be. This highlighted the conflict of interest within CAS itself as a tribunal run by the very sporting bodies it is meant to arbitrate. As such, the 2018 regulation would stay in effect. Caster appealed to the Federal Supreme Court of Switzerland, but this too was rejected. Ultimately, Caster would go all the way to the European Court of Human Rights, where she would win on the basis of an infringement of her human rights and having been discriminated against. This ruling, however, was only related to the *process* to which she was subjected, not the policy itself. As such, the IAAF was able to hold firm on implementing this version of its policy.

Mirroring the approach that the IAAF had taken with women with high testosterone, in 2015 the IOC updated its policy regulating trans women in women's sport. The IOC had allowed trans women to participate in women's sport since 2004, however that version of the policy had required surgical anatomical changes as a condition of participation. The 2015 version removed the requirement for surgery, recognizing that this may be a human rights violation, and imposed a testosterone-level restriction. Under this new policy, trans women had to reduce and maintain their testosterone levels to below 10 nmol/l of blood for at least twelve months before competition.

These policies ultimately imposed indelible harm on the women athletes subjected to them. We know that at least four women athletes from Global South countries have been subjected to coerced, unnecessary surgery on the basis of IAAF policies: surgeries that left them permanently sick and unable to function, let alone compete.[18] These women have since shared, in a damning Human Rights Watch report on the human rights abuses in sex testing of women athletes, that they were not fully informed as to the purpose and intention of these medically unnecessary surgeries (which they had been flown to France to undergo). The Human Rights Watch report has, further, documented many other stories and impacts on the women athletes subjected to these policies.[19]

Similarly, Canadian cyclist Kristen Worley, a trans woman, won her human rights case against the IOC on the basis that the surgery and the lowered testosterone levels the IOC had required her to undergo to participate had been medically unnecessary and an abuse of her human rights. She too has been left with lasting medical problems.

The World Medical Association (WMA) has come out strongly against the medico-scientific regulation of women athletes. It has called on its members to have no part in implementing these policies, on medico-ethical and human rights grounds. In particular, it has stated that it is unethical for a physician to alter a patient's body for the sole purposes of sport. As such, the WMA has, in no uncertain terms, called for the withdrawal of these regulations.

Tanner Scale, and more

The early 2020s have seen sports organizations become obsessed with the regulation of women athletes to an extent that we have never seen before. The greatest gender equality that we've ever had is being met with the harshest backlash we've ever experienced. Sport for women (and women's space in the world) has clearly become too big for its boots, and the need to police womanhood is stronger than ever. Gatekeeping of *Women's Sport* and notions of 'needing' to define who is a 'real' woman is at an all-time high. With the increasing visibility and acceptance of even wider forms of not only womanhood but personhood itself, patriarchal control has gone into overdrive.

There is no better example than the control World Aquatics has decided it needs to assert. In June 2022 World Aquatics voted through a 'Policy on Eligibility for the Men's and Women's

Competition Categories'. This new policy had been developed because the IOC had, in 2021, rescinded its 2015 policy regulating trans athletes (and athletes with differences of sex development) and had instead brought in guidelines that ultimately devolved decision- and policy-making down to individual sports on the basis that regulation should be done on a sport-by-sport basis, if indeed it was needed at all. World Aquatics decided – we suspect in large part in response to Lia Thomas competing (as we discussed in Chapter Two) – that a policy was needed. The result was, in a nutshell, that the new World Aquatics policy required:

- that *all* athletes in the women's category undergo (i) a chromosomal test to 'certify their chromosomal sex', and
- for those athletes who fall under further scrutiny, possible further medical assessment. This requires not only (ii) blood testosterone-level testing but (iii) androgen sensitivity testing, and (iv) a screen to determine level of pubertal development.

This should sound familiar. The first three elements of this new policy will now be recognizable to readers (who will now also be familiar with the flaws and critiques of each of these approaches). The fourth element is a return to the old nude parade, just under a different, more scientific-sounding name. To ensure we grasp the full picture, let's look at each of the elements in turn.

i. Chromosome testing

We have already discussed the reasons why chromosomal testing was phased out by World Athletics (the new name for IAAF) and the IOC in the early 2000s: it is not conclusive, is humiliating and was objected to by women athletes. But in 2023 World Aquatics decided to overlook all this and forge ahead regardless with the return of chromosomal testing, testosterone limits and androgen sensitivity testing. The federation does, however, clearly recognize the unreliability of these forms of testing because it has now included provision for a new part of its eligibility criteria: pubertal development screening. In the policy, this is comprised of the Tanner Scale.

ii. Blood testosterone level and limits

World Aquatics has set a new limit on blood testosterone levels at a shockingly low 2.5 nanomoles per litre of blood for relevant women. We saw this new lower limit introduced by UCI (Union Cycliste Internationale, the international governing body for cycling) recently too. Importantly, this new limit is down from the 10 nmol/l of the IOC in 2016, and 5 nmol/l of World Athletics in 2018. How can we not assume that these limits are completely arbitrary? We discussed earlier how there is little evidence for the link between endogenous testosterone and sporting performance, and women can and do have much higher natural testosterone levels than this.

Further, testosterone is not the 'elixir of performance' as many would have us believe. As Jordan-Young and Karkazis explain: 'testosterone is not the "master molecule of athleticism". A high natural testosterone level does not simply translate into medals. In addition, we now know that there are people whose bodies cannot use testosterone, even if they do have high testosterone levels.'[20] So, to mitigate this complication, World Aquatics had to include an assessment of whether a relevant athlete's body can use testosterone. And this is where it gets even more concerning.

iii. Androgen (testosterone) sensitivity assessment

We mentioned androgen sensitivity testing before, but we haven't yet discussed how, rather than being a scientific test, this is a much-critiqued subjective process. There is no reproducible, valid laboratory test for whether or not someone's body can use testosterone. As such, this assessment involves, for example, a doctor undertaking radiological imaging of internal organs, and assessing and measuring the development and size of the clitoris, breasts and pubic hair. These assessments, particularly that of clitoral size, are widely viewed as 'inappropriate, subject to false interpretation, and an invasion of personal privacy'.[21] The mere suggestion that girls and women should have to undergo these invasive checks to participate in sport should be a concern to us all. Sports organizations mandating this is somewhat outrageous.

iv. Tanner Stage 2 assessment

Finally, the World Aquatics policy mandates an assessment of whether a relevant athlete in the women's category (trans girls and women, and women with sex variations) has undergone any part of what they call 'male puberty'. This shift to a focus on 'male puberty' (or androgenization) is a new one, representing a move away from testosterone (seemingly because the use of testosterone as a proxy for advantage has been widely critiqued). The way they intend to assess 'male puberty' (a misnomer in and of itself) is via the Tanner Scale.

However, the Tanner Scale is yet again a critiqued subjective scale in which physicians assess external primary and secondary sex characteristics such as the size of the breasts and clitoris, pubic hair and/or, relevant to trans girls and women, testicular volume. Let us say this in a different way: they intend to have a look to see whether a relevant girl or woman is beyond stage I or II on the Tanner chart (which is a series of pictures of girls and boys at various stages of pubertal development) to decide whether they have an advantage in sport. This is hardly scientific of them, especially when this only applies to those athletes who fall under scrutiny. The Tanner Scale has now essentially become the new proxy for supposed advantage in sport.

It should come as no surprise that Tanner Scale assessment is not reliable, and open to subjectivity. A woman with a sex variation that means she has a large clitoris could 'fail' this test. A cis-woman with a large clitoris could 'fail' this test. Trans women are reduced down to what their genitalia look like (and it seems that World Athletics expects trans women's genitalia to all conform to the 'male' side of this binary scale, betraying a stark lack of awareness of trans bodies). Similarly to androgen sensitivity assessment above, it is inappropriate, subject to false interpretation and an invasion of personal privacy.

As sociologist Celia Roberts has shown, the scale was developed in the 1950s and '60s using disadvantaged White children in England as subjects, without ethical approval or consent (egregiously, the standard in scientific methods at the time). This small set of very specific children now represent a notion of what is considered 'normal'. Roberts describes how Susan Euling and colleagues concluded that the Tanner Scale 'should not be taken as typical for non-white children, who are today seen as notably "different"'.[22] Anyone who does not conform thus ends up constituting 'compelling "mysteries" for contemporary biomedicine and technoscience', Roberts states. Eligibility policies, in this way, result in not only gendered but racialized and ableist outcomes too. It is important to understand that '[r]ather than a neutral scientific tool, the Tanner Scale is a significant actor in the making of modern sexed bodies.'[23] It is no wonder that Women of Colour and Black women, like Dutee Chand and Caster Semenya respectively, 'failed' gender verification screenings. The standard is all wrong and far too simplistic.

Sports have now shifted the goalposts for assessing whether or not someone in the women's category has undergone 'male puberty'; but make no mistake, this approach and concept is just as nebulous and subjective as the approaches that came before it. This type of policy remains a deeply problematic and racist 'nude parade' under the guise of scientism and medical paternalism. As Sharda Ugra writes, this type of approach 'escalates . . . "eligibility regulations for female classification" from medico-scientific decoy into what it really is: the abuse of the rights of women athletes to privacy, dignity and health'.[24]

Privacy, dignity and health

As the journalist Frankie de la Cretaz has argued, sex testing, in the guise of protecting women, actually strips them of bodily autonomy.[25] What looks like an attack only on trans athletes in reality affects all women and girls in sport. Sex testing normalizes the erasure of bodily autonomy and privacy, which is connected to the increased potential for sexual abuse. Frankie explains how the kinds of policies that we have described in this chapter normalize the practice of girls and women being asked to give up their privacy by: 1) showing genitalia to people in power (via nude parades/

gender verification/Tanner Scale assessments); and 2) providing sensitive medical information to sports organizations (via gender verification procedures/chromosome tests/PCR tests/testosterone level tests). It is impossible to refuse to undergo sex testing, particularly as the power imbalance between the athlete and her coach/doctor/club/national squad/international federation is so greatly skewed towards the latter. She has to conform and submit, giving up her bodily autonomy and privacy (which is often already significantly corroded due to the very nature of being someone who sacrifices their body at the altar of sport). And once she does, her last remaining power is taken from her. She is at the mercy of the sporting organization, who could at any moment take her sporting career away on the whim of a policy decision. Karkazis and Carpenter describe these as 'impossible "choices"'.[26]

In Cretaz's view, this athlete is now primed for sexual abuse. Her privacy, dignity and bodily autonomy have been taken from her, leaving her vulnerable to grooming and exploitation. We elaborate more on this in the next chapter. Human Rights Watch has already shown in its report how sex testing practices are forms of physical and psychological abuse, and the IOC consensus statement on harassment and abuse in sport explains how tests are gateways for sexual abuse.[27] Sport is a context ripe for the sexual exploitation of girls and women, and we will discuss the appalling Larry Nassar case in the next chapter. Sex testing practices are only increasing the susceptibility of those who are most vulnerable. These policies, rather than making sport safer for them, place girls and women at risk.

It can be easy to dismiss these concerns as only being related to elite sport settings, which we hear should be regulated to ensure 'fairness' or 'safety'. However, it is important to know that the rise of anti-trans legislation in the USA and elsewhere (under the guise of 'saving women's sports') is attempting to mandate sex testing for all sports participation, from school to grassroots to amateur to elite. Indeed, we have already seen legislation tabled in Georgia that aims to create 'genitalia assessment boards' to assess student athletes. Eroding the medical and personal privacy and bodily autonomy of young people who want to participate in sport, by subjecting them to this kind of assessment, should be a red line for us all.

In the context of teenage girls already participating in far less sport and physical activity than their boy counterparts, sex testing is never going to increase their involvement (despite the story that we might be sold that this somehow makes sport 'safer and fairer' for girls and women). Exercising one's physical capabilities is an extremely important element of health and flourishing (as we'll discuss in Chapter Four) and creating humiliating barriers for girls and women is not how we make sport safer and more welcoming for them.

The hyper focus on sex testing as *the* solution to 'saving women's sport' overlooks and masks the actual problems that beset *Women's Sport*: unequal pay and prize money, lack of access to high-quality resources and training, over-representation of men in coaching and leadership, and harassment and abuse, not to mention the ways in which testing creates a fixation on sex-separation as supposedly the only way in which we can make sport safe and fair for all (we will discuss this more, including alternative ways of conceptualizing sport, in Chapter Five). The focus on sex testing drains not only resources – that is, from what we could be doing about these real problems – but our ability to think expansively about what we want the future of sport to be.

The definition of woman

In this chapter, through a history of failed attempts to verify sex, we have shown that defining woman, for the purposes of sport or anything else, is far from a simple matter. Doesn't this leave us with a problem? Our book is about women in sport but, so far, we have not been able to say what a woman is. Should this be seen as a fundamental flaw?

We don't think that it is. The demands for a simple definition of woman have proved such a definition demonstrably impossible. No one can say in a sentence what it is to be a woman, or a man, in a way that covers all people and separates them correctly into two groups. Instead, we should accept that woman is an irreducibly complex, socially constructed category, which is usually coupled with an attempt to impose a strict (gender) binary on human beings who do not divide so neatly. However, this complexity does not mean that the term is without good use. After all, no one can really define a chair either: we cannot provide a simple set of conditions that are satisfied by all and only the things that are chairs. Nevertheless, we can all talk about chairs and identify chairs with a high degree of success. There could be some cases where it is unclear whether something is a chair or not. But that is fine. We can say much the same about the word 'woman' because, as we have seen, any attempt to identify a single marker of sex (genitals, chromosomes, testosterone levels) is bound to fail. We now know that language does not work with strict definitions: what philosophers have called necessary and sufficient conditions. The failure to find them in the case of woman is not so significant when the same can be said of most other concepts and categories.

When is a woman too good to be a woman? In this chapter, we have discussed how the policing of women's bodies is codified and formalized through sport, and that this is designed to keep women small. We continued our argument through from Chapter Two, showing that when it became obvious that the manufactured category of *Women's Sport* was not as effective at keeping women in their place as patriarchy would have liked, a new method for control emerged: policing women's bodies.

Sex testing in modern sport has an eighty-year history, undergoing many iterations, a number of which we have detailed above. Some of these approaches have been discarded, others recycled. But they all have one aim in common: these so-called 'female eligibility policies' ultimately police the purity of what a woman 'should' be. Isn't it always about policing bodies, and thus society? It was never about 'fairness' or giving women a chance, it was about control. The policing and exclusion/segregation of some women and girls in sport ultimately places in danger all women and girls, and this is why it is no feminist position to support it.

4

Being in Your Body

If sport is a patriarchal institution, should women and queer people have anything to do with it at all? Might they choose to pass it by, seek no involvement, opt out? A lot of women and queer people have done precisely this, and for understandable reasons. Participation rates remain lower for girls and women than for boys and men in most sports worldwide. When Sport England published its biannual Active Lives survey in May 2019, it announced it had found lower participation of women than men across all sports, with 313,600 fewer women than men being regularly active. Indeed, nearly 40 per cent of women were getting insufficient exercise to enjoy the health benefits. Nevertheless, 13 million women said that they would like to do more sport and exercise but, as well as lack of time, cited fear of judgement and low confidence as reasons they did not participate. In fandom, too, women and queer people are involved less. Most sports fans are men.

Given what we have seen in the foregoing chapters, it is perfectly reasonable for those who have been locked out of an activity to take little interest in it. It also makes sense that those people are put off participating because of low confidence and a fear of being judged for taking part. Like many domains that were traditionally gatekept by men for men, it makes sense that women and queer people dismiss sport as a pursuit that at best offers little or nothing for them, and at worst is actively harmful to them. As a 2015 review in *Sociology Compass* by sports sociologist Ramón Spaaij and colleagues showed, sport has been institutionalized across lines of gender, race, nation and social mobility, the result of which is that sport upholds social hierarchies, and is not very welcoming to those who challenge the status quo.[1]

We have seen in the previous chapters that sport has always been the domain of men, and women's exclusion is par for the course. The status quo is policed on two fronts: through the creation of the inferior *Women's Sport* category, and then regulating who is a 'real' woman for the purposes of this category. These are hurdles that people in *Sport* itself (men's sport) never have to overcome. Given this strict, harmful policing, it is understandable, then, that so many women and queer people (anyone, really, who is marginalized) opt out of sport and exercise.

Nevertheless, the thought that this is inevitable can be resisted. Our purpose in this book is to advocate instead for a vision of *Feminist Sport* that is safe and welcoming for all. Chapter Six will make our case for what this will look like, but for now we focus on why it matters. We make the case for *Feminist Sport* on the grounds that sport ought to be a positive good in anyone's life. We argue that sport, as an organized, institutional form of game playing, in which we aim to exercise our physical abilities to their optimum extent, is an indispensable part of a good, fulfilling human life. This is about more than just practical health benefits but concerns a happy life more generally.

Patriarchy has reserved these goods for those whom it serves. And, in doing so, it has created man as superior and dominant, and woman as inferior and subordinate in ways that are about far more than sport alone. It has also erased anyone who is gender expansive. Just as we have seen a shift in our understanding in the last fifty years – that women's brains aren't smaller and less capable than men's are – the same shift can happen in our understanding of men's and women's bodies. Then we can go further, moving beyond the binary altogether, as will be seen in Chapter Five.

This chapter makes the case that physical activity is a human good for all, maybe even a right, because it can be a benefit to all. Sport should be, therefore, a safe, welcoming space for everyone.

Socially constructed sport

Let us put some flesh on these bones and explain why sport matters for everyone. Our argument centres on the role of sport in a good human life and, in particular, the nature of embodiment and the satisfaction to be found in exercising our physical capacities or abilities. Many of the same arguments relate to our mental capacities too, but those are not our immediate concern here.

We first cannot avoid considering the question of what sport is. It is far from easy to define sport, as we saw with the concepts of both 'woman' and 'chair', and any definition will be controversial. Strict definitions are not always possible. It is crucial nevertheless that we explain how we see sport, since only then can we describe its role in the good human life.

Sport, in our view, is the institutionalized form of games. Games themselves are a more formal manifestation of pure play, with a more codified set of rules. Sport involves even more codification and formalization. The modern concept of sport emerged only in the nineteenth century, at the same time as the possibility of its commercial exploitation. This was partly due to social changes and partly due to industrial advances. Once we understood how to build stadiums and charge an entry fee, and then developed an accompanying sports media, the financial possibilities of sport led to its rapid development and professionalization.

Sport is thus a social construction. People have always run, jumped and thrown things, and may even have done so for pleasure or what was commonly called recreation. They may have done some of these activities competitively in ancient Games or medieval archery contests. Only once we had governing bodies and associations, however, did we have social institutions capable of deeming certain forms of activity *Sport*. On this institutional theory of sport, the term is an honorific that a group of various vested interests bestow upon some activities and not others. Track and Field has the status of sport. Chess does not. Parkour did not have the status of being a sport until 2017, when the UK became the first country worldwide to recognize it as such. The mechanisms for the bestowal of this status are mainly informal, though they can involve formal bodies. Discussions occur among these various sporting (and other) vested interests until an adequate consensus has been reached between them. An important such sporting institution, for instance, is the IOC. When an activity such as BMX biking is accepted into the Olympics, as it was in 2020, it is a major indicator that the activity is deemed to be a sport as it has agreed to institute the regulations needed to be one. And, once it is counted as a sport, many additional commercial opportunities follow.

One thing that makes an activity specifically sport, rather than another kind of activity, is that its institutions – governing bodies, agencies, national centres, media interests and so on – developed around physical contests. This is where a deeper analysis of the human condition is possible, especially one that highlights the significance of embodiment and physical ability.

While many of the things we do for sport we could also do out of necessity, such as running as fast as we can from danger, in a sporting context we do them primarily for their own sake. As philosopher Bernard Suits describes in *The Grasshopper*, a game is a voluntary attempt to overcome unnecessary obstacles.[2] Games are ultimately ends in themselves, done for the satisfaction they bring, rather than for some other end. That we do unnecessary things in sport shows that we accept them as ends in themselves rather than as a means for something else. We do them so that we can play the sport, since there is no sport unless we abide by its constitutive rules. Hence, in the high jump, if the point was merely to get to the other side of the bar, it would be easier to walk under it rather than jump over it. Instead, we accept this unnecessary obstacle: to get to the other side *by jumping over*. Furthermore, the aim of the sport is to get over as high a bar as you possibly can.

We see this pattern in all other sports: this acceptance of unnecessary obstacles. Another way of putting it is that in order to count as playing the sport, you must accept a less efficient means of achieving your goal over a more efficient, or easier, means. In golf, if the aim were simply to get the ball in the hole, the easiest way would be by carrying the ball and putting it in there with your hand. Instead, you have to get it in using a set of clubs, taking as few strokes as possible. In races, such as the 200 metres, one might be able to get to the finishing line first by cutting across the centre of the sports field, or by tripping up your opponents. But the aim is to get to the line while staying in your assigned lane. If one cuts across the grass, you have effectively stopped playing the sport.

One might think that one seeks to jump the highest, run the fastest or take the fewest golf shots as a means to an end: namely, to become rich and famous. But this really only applies to elite sport, where the riches are gained by a tiny minority. Most of us are not playing sport for that reason. Nor does it explain the satisfaction in achieving a personal best in a sport: one that comes nowhere near winning a prize. In the London Marathon, for instance, there are thousands of runners who know that they have no chance of winning the race but they still could be deeply satisfied by registering their best time. The rewards of sport are not primarily financial, then, and we would argue that even those who do get such rewards are primarily engaged with the sport for other reasons. Would one really become the best swimmer in the world, for instance, if one was doing it just for fame and wealth? No, there are other ways to achieve that. One is primarily doing it because one loves swimming. Being very good at it will usually only increase that love.

Capabilities

This brings us to what sport really means and why everyone, including, of course, women and queer people, should want to do it. The central idea is that it is pleasurable, rewarding and fulfilling to exercise one's capabilities, especially to their optimum extent, and this is because our physical abilities are such an integral part of our embodiment and the human condition more generally. To be in your body is not simply to passively occupy a space: simply

to be. It is to be physically empowered: to be able to do things –
to run, jump, throw, hit, push, kick, catch, hold, carry, balance,
endure, aim, tumble, reach, swim and so on. To enjoy being in
one's body, one exercises these abilities. Furthermore, sport is a
space that encourages and develops the exercise of these physical abilities. Hence, for many, it is a simple pleasure to jump, a
greater pleasure to master a technique for high jumping, and the
greatest pleasure to jump to the very best of one's ability. In sport
one can discover the extent of such abilities: just how fast one
can run or how accurately one can hit a target. Some sports even
allow perfect outcomes, such as a perfect bowling game, a nine-
dart finish, maximum points for skating. These require complete
mastery of the ability.

A philosophical idea that connects with this aspect of sport is
Martha Nussbaum's capabilities approach to human flourishing.[3]
What philosophers often call *the good life* cannot be gauged simply
by how rich one is or how happy one feels. To rest content with
what one is given, and not explore other opportunities that could
enrich one's life further, is not enough for most of us. Nussbaum
instead sees flourishing as a matter of developing one's capabilities so that one is constantly growing as a person. If one doesn't
speak Mandarin, one might think there is no point in learning
to do so. Once people have that ability, however, they can both
take pleasure in being able to do something new – in having that
power – and have a greater degree of freedom than someone who
cannot speak the language. Our speaker is now free to converse
with many more people in their own language, for instance, while
our monoglot English speaker has no such liberty.

Likewise in the case of sport. Someone who is capable of
swimming all four strokes has greater freedom than someone

who can swim only one, and this second swimmer has more free-dom than someone who cannot swim at all. Someone who has learnt to dive properly into water now has that option open to them, where previously they had not. The connection between capability and freedom is brought out clearly in the following case: when you can jump 2 metres high, you can also jump every height less than that. If you can jump only 1 metre high, then you have only half of those possibilities open to you and thus have half the freedom, in respect of high jumping, of someone who can jump the two.

The existentialist philosophers, particularly Simone de Beauvoir, sometimes made use of a notion of *becoming* in which we did not really have a fixed being or essence but were, ideally, in a constant state of growth, developing all the time, learning new skills and new knowledge, changing always. Sport gives us an opportunity for physical becoming. One has the same body one always had, in one sense, but we can nevertheless enter a process of becoming by acquiring new or different physical abilities and honing them until they reach their optimum. One might never reach that ideal end point, but the idea of becoming is that one can still undertake the journey, never reaching a conclusion but always travelling.

It is in this context that we argue for sport that is inclusive for all: that has a set of values that make for a safe and welcom-ing space for everyone. Sport develops our physical being, puts us in tune with – allowing us to gain mastery of and through – our bodies. It is a pleasure and a joy to exercise such mastery, to execute a physical skill to one's optimum level. In doing so, our being is fully physically integrated. We make the most of our embodiment.

Socially constructed bodies

Two cases require further comment. We are about to proceed to the specific case of women's bodies, since there have been damaging arguments in the past that this view of embodiment, in which we should develop our physical capacities as fully as possible, cannot be applied to women. Before that, however, we should consider the question of disability in sport and anticipate an objection that the capabilities approach to physical flourishing unjustly centres on able-bodied people to the exclusion of disabled people and disability sports.

We do not think it does, however, since the same considerations apply to everyone, regardless of their body. Even a beginner enjoys learning new physical skills through sport and the 'becoming' of improving those skills. The assertion that it is pleasurable to develop a new skill is not sensitive to the level at which one starts, or the maximum level one can reach. Disability may place constraints on athletes in respect of some physical skills (in respect of other skills, it might not at all). The rise of disability or adapted sports, although too slow and not well-enough funded, shows that many disabled people can and do enjoy their physical being and are in their bodies just as much as the rest of us. Indeed, perhaps sport can play an even more important role for disabled people since they are mostly disabled by societal barriers, not their body itself.

The social conception of disability allows us to go beyond thinking of physical impairment as the key factor in disability. On the social model, disability is itself socially constructed since the world (our built environment, social arrangements and even ideas about what disabled people can and can't do) is built by and for able-bodied people. The social model allows us to recognize that by building a more inclusive world, disabled people will have more independence, choice and control. An inclusive model of sport (*Feminist Sport*) is one which is constructed and organized differently, so as to be safe and welcoming for all.

This brings us to the second case that requires comment, and here we will be more detailed. This is, of course, women and queer people in sport. However, what we have said in respect of sport and disability has some resonance here since being a woman is also a category that is socially constructed, including through our relationship to sport. And this sport has been built by men, primarily for men.

We have so far in this chapter presented a positive vision of what sport should be: what sport should be for everyone. It presents the possibility for us to be at ease with our physical embodiment, enjoying our bodies and our development of the physical skills that are useful in various sports. Anyone who is not a cis, straight, White, able-bodied man is rarely afforded this mastery, however.

In a patriarchal world, women's bodies are presented as delicate and wholly unsuitable for sport. It is not wide of the mark to associate such views with the Victorian era. This may sound outdated, but such narratives have been all-too persistent into the present day (now draped in scientism as we saw in Chapters Two and Three). Men and women are considered almost different species, particularly when it comes to their physicality. We saw Ernest Mason's views in the previous chapter, where we also touched on those of Frederick Hollick, and his 1847 book *The Diseases of Woman*. Hollick's chapter on hysteria, an affliction supposedly experienced only by women, makes it clear that he saw women, what they do, and their bodies, as the problem:

It [hysteria] is also most common between puberty and the change of life, but is nevertheless found in quite young girls, and in old women. Young persons just about being regulated are very subject to it, and those who have deranged menstruation, also widows, those who have no children, and those in whom the change of life is about to take place. Some of the immediate causes are, the first period, suppressed menstruation, late marriage, chronic inflammation of the womb, vicious habits, and long continued constipation.[4]

That meant just about every woman! Despite some of these causes being social in origin (marriage, for instance), it was clear that there was no escaping hysteria since ultimately it is women's biology that is responsible:

In regard to the starting point, or original seat of Hysteria, there seems to be no doubt of its being in the Uterus, which becomes subject to a peculiar excitement, or disturbance, that exerts a wonderful sympathetic influence on the whole system. The Uterus, it must be remembered, is the controlling organ in the female body.[5]

The name for this women's 'disease' (as with hysterectomy), comes from the Latin for womb. If one has this kind of attitude towards women's bodies to begin with, it is hardly too great a leap to consider them as troublesome and generally unsuitable for any 'real' activity, including sport.

The uterus has remained a particular preoccupation. As recently as 2010, Gian-Franco Kasper, president of the International

Ski Federation, suggested that women should not be allowed to compete in the ski jump due to the danger that their uteruses could burst upon landing. According to Kathleen McCrone, in her book *Playing the Game: Sport and the Physical Emancipation of English Women, 1870–1914*, the myth of the falling uterus became prevalent specifically as a way to keep women out of sport and away from any physical exertion.[6] What is more surprising is just how long the myth has persisted despite a lack of any scientific basis. A connection with the reproductive faculties of women is no coincidence, however, as the primary purpose of woman in a patriarchal society is her reproductive role. She is primed, prized and praised for her potential for motherhood. The idea that sport – the peak of which often coincides with when she is most fertile (ages 18–35) – could lead to infertility is thus used as a convenient and powerful disincentive to participate. And so patriarchal control continues. Understanding how patriarchy works helps us to understand what today seems bizarre, and why men have never been subjected to the same fear despite their testicles, since they are external, being far more vulnerable. This was finally acknowledged in a 2002 IOC Medical Commission report, which states that 'The female reproductive organs are better protected from serious athletic injury than the male organs.'[7]

The point is that a conflict is posed between motherhood and sports participation while it is never made with fatherhood. First, fertility in the form of menstruation is depicted as the ultimate marker of fragility, as pervasive ideas about the menstrual cycle being linked with injury abound. Instead of seeing the menstrual cycle as a healthy, normal aspect of life (as it is seen in some non-Western cultures, for example, Māori), sport has demanded control of it. Practice has traditionally focused on halting the menstrual cycle, intentionally or unintentionally. Visibly menstruating in public is considered one of the ultimate taboos. Women's unruly hormonal bodies must be brought in line to be more like men's if they are to be athletes, while – curiously – the fact that men have hormonal cycles too is conveniently ignored. In recent years we have moved more towards biohacking the 'female body', with research seeking to find the best ways to track menstrual cycles and then optimize training and injury prevention around them (despite there being no evidence that this will make a difference; this practice also again places a hyper-focus on the 'female body' as the hormonal *other*). We have already discussed how so-called 'period smoothies' are on offer to prevent injuries (while men get protein shakes).

If an athlete happens to fall pregnant, she is then treated as if she is incapacitated, with her contracts and sponsorships and sports participation halted. American Track and Field athletes Allyson Felix and Alysia Montaño have both spoken openly in the *New York Times* about their loss of compensation from their sponsor Nike after they became pregnant. This led to a public outcry and eventually a congressional hearing in 2019, after which Nike agreed to new contracts guaranteeing pay and bonuses for athletes for 18 months around their pregnancy. Workplace protections are in place to prevent this kind of discrimination in other fields. In any case, physical activity is safe, appropriate and desirable for most pregnant people, and many athletes can and do successfully compete while pregnant. Famously, images of Alysia Montaño competing while pregnant are available online. Then, when an athlete becomes a mother, she is always depicted through that lens. She is asked who is taking care of her children while she is competing, a question that would never be asked of a father. The assumption is clear: fertility, birthing and care of any children is womanhood's primary focus in a patriarchal world. Any woman seeking to be an athlete is placing not only herself in jeopardy, but humankind, and must be protected from herself. And when she is an athlete, her reproductive capacity and status as a woman becomes a problem, an impediment to participation. To be an athlete is, once again, incompatible with womanhood.

We do not discount a possible individual effect on performance from menstruation. What we reject, however, is the hyper-focus on and exploitation of biology, or even supposed biology, in the creation of a mythic fragility and, ultimately, a pretext for women's supposed inferiority in sport. The formal barriers to excellence are easy to document. We have already catalogued explicit bans and female eligibility regulations. What can be even more powerful, more effective and more pernicious are the informal, cultural blocks to women's full inclusion. Mythic feminine fragility is one such cultural factor, which works by persuading women themselves that participation is against their own best interests. We have argued, on the contrary, that participation in sport is a good, and so it ought to be a human right if we think that all people should be allowed to flourish.

Where patriarchy wishes us to accept a negative narrative concerning women's bodies, we can see how self-fulfilling such a narrative will be, since it sends women's participation in sport into a negative spiral. If women think that their bodies are not as suited to sport as men's are, then they will become involved in lower numbers, accept easier options, aim at smaller goals and their performances will trail behind those of men. The next generation then see this, assume the performance gap between men and women is inevitable, and participate even less. The divisions between men and women will only increase. Instead, we wish to replace the negative spiral with a positive one. Like anyone else's, women's embodiment should be seen as an opportunity for development. This embodiment is a perfectly serviceable foundation for the development of physical achievements. Instead of a focus on what women's bodies can't do, which already feeds the negative narrative, let us concentrate on what women can do. Let us give young women the same aspirations that we give to young men. Don't begin from a position that women will always, naturally, be second best. There is, after all, no solid reason to believe that this is true. It would be wholly spurious to make this assessment on the basis of relative achievements within current, patriarchal arrangements, since women's social inequality has been deliberately turned into a physical inequality. Let us first create a gender-equal society, and then we might eventually be in a position to see just how far women can go and how close their sporting performances will be to those of men. And then let's go further, beyond the binary (as we will discuss in Chapter Five).

Under such arrangements, as we touched on in the previous chapter, the manufactured moral panic regarding trans athletes will also be disarmed. That trans women are seen as a threat to women in sport, through gaining an unfair advantage, itself rests on a view that men and women have natural differences and men are naturally stronger than women. In reality, participation rates in sport for trans people lag far behind those of cis people. Nor would it be safe to assume that trans women have the same average physical attributes as cis men. More and more transphobic rulings from sporting bodies will act only to exclude this already marginalized population from sport even further. Especially among young people, at an age when sporting participation is seen as a good, and an important part of personal development, being trans means you are unlikely to be attracted to sports. Even where some are able to persevere and overcome those informal barriers, they are now being met by formal ones.

Queering sports

Emerging as an alternative to both *Sport* and *Women's Sport*, with their institutionalized and enforced gender binary, people have sometimes exercised the option of queering sporting spaces. We will present two examples: roller derby and pole dancing.

Roller derby grew out of the popularity of roller skating – mainly in the United States – and saw organized competitions evolve in the 1930s. The nature and rules of the sport were constantly developing, often with theatrical elements introduced. For a time, once TV coverage arrived, it became semi-choreographed, like wrestling sometimes is. While such elements may seem anathema to the idea of sport, since it means that the outcomes are to an extent prearranged, the theatrical side could also be seen as rather integral to the sport since putting on a show was part of the attraction. Ballroom dancing also has this combination of the theatrical and competitive, in which one aims to win but also look magnificent while doing so. This form of roller derby was played on banked tracks, predominantly as a form of sports entertainment.

The 2000s saw a re-emergence of roller derby, but this time with less of a focus on the theatrical element and more on the athleticism. Modern roller derby is a contact sport, contested by two teams of fifteen skaters, on an oval track. Its flavour, however, remains less organized sport and more do-it-yourself grassroots. Importantly, contemporary roller derby was mainly revived by women and the sport has a strong punk aesthetic and third-wave feminist ethic. It is this feminist underpinning, grounded in principles such as intersectionality, sex positivity, ecofeminism and transfeminism, that has set roller derby aside from traditional *Sport* and even *Women's Sport* as we know it. Roller derby today is unapologetically queer: participants actively reject how things 'should' be done. In rejecting heteronormativity, the sex binary and social norms, roller derby has queered sport by making it a space in which women and queer people are able to be their full selves, free from the constraints of societal expectations. It is no coincidence, then, that derby is one of the few sports that has always been trans inclusive. It is also, in the open category, the only contact sport than can be played by men and women (and anyone) together.

Today roller derby has more competitive credibility. But also it is a sport that chooses to exist at the margins, with the status of sport not quite fully bestowed. It was among eight new events considered for inclusion at the 2020 Olympics but was not eventually selected, mainly because it refuses to conform to the institutionalized rules and regulations of sport, in which it might be relegated to an inferior and regulated *Women's Sport* in a patriarchal world.[8]

Another queer sport of this kind is pole dancing. While pole dancing has historical origins dating back eight hundred years, developing from sporting and performance activities in India, China and Egypt, contemporary pole dancing emerged out of spaces in which sex workers performed erotic dance. In the 1980s pole dancing developed as an activity incorporating athletic climbs, spins and inversions into erotic dance routines. American Fawnia Mondey became the first recognized pole dancing instructor, as we know it today, teaching the activity as an art. This form of pole dancing has grown exponentially while staying true to its roots. Because it grew out of erotic dance and burlesque, most often performed in tents and bars, it has always had a subversive, countercultural essence. Pole dancing of this kind is an unapologetically queer space in which women and queer people are able to safely be their full selves, free from the constraints of societal expectations, while exercising their full capacities in feats that require enormous physicality, especially upper body strength (a strength we too often hear is not available to women).

By 2009, the pole dancing community had split, however. In that year the International Pole Sports Federation was formed with the express intention of washing pole dancing of its erotic dance roots and rebranding it as a sport. Pole Sports, or Pole Fitness as it is sometimes also called, would focus on recrafting the activity into a non-sexual sport, in the same vein as gymnastics. The ultimate goal was to develop the activity into a sport that could be institutionalized through rules and regulations, and eventually into an Olympic Sport.

It should come as no surprise that the two sides of the pole dancing community, with their different values, see their futures in very different ways. Pole dancing sees itself as an art, is proud of its roots in sex work and erotic dance, and is shamelessly and defiantly queer. A *Feminist Sport*. Pole Sports, on the other hand, seeks to gain acceptance within the mainstream. It seeks a clear break from its roots, and aims to be conventional. These aims cater to an ultimate goal of recognition as a sport (or, more likely, a *Women's Sport*), with all the corresponding rules and regulations within a patriarchal world. One rejects the status quo; the other upholds it.

Both roller derby and pole dance constitute a set of counter-cultural physical activities, designed primarily for women and queer people, by women and queer people. Even though these sports do not have the attention and riches of some others, the attraction is clear: safety, acceptance and the opportunity to exercise physical abilities without the constraints of manhood and womanhood.

Sport and *Women's Sport* as we know them uphold strict notions of manhood and womanhood. *Feminist Sport* rejects and destroys them. We are, as we'll discuss in Chapter Six, for *Feminist Sport*. As Angela Saini has shown in her book *Inferior*, in a patriarchal world, those in power choose the criteria on which they can make and remake their superiority.[9] In the case of *Sport* and *Women's Sport*, the former creates and upholds the physical strength and power of men, while the latter creates and reinforces the grace and beauty (and supposed lack of physical strength and power) of women. *Sport* is given more prestige and resources than *Women's Sport*, and then we are told that women will simply never be as good as men. This is how patriarchy defends itself.

Countercultural, *Feminist Sport* refutes this. There is a very much deliberate distancing of these sports from the patriarchal order, and thus masculine and feminine ideals. Queer sports open up a window to a different way of thinking about sport, what we want it to be and who we want it to serve. We'll discuss this more in Chapter Six.

Abuse

The problems women face in what is currently *Women's Sport* are innumerable. We have discussed the ways in which women (and queer people) are excluded culturally by dominant norms of what a sporting body is and what a woman's body is. This imposes a fundamental incompatibility between being a woman and playing sport. We have also mentioned many of the formal barriers women have faced historically and continue to face. Equality is far from achieved in sport, as in wider society. If we want to see the sheer scale of the problem still remaining, however, it is instructive to look at the abuse that women in mainstream sport face for daring to intrude into this man's world.

The on-field and on-television post-match celebrations following Spain's Football World Cup win of 2023 quickly became a political scandal. For years, Spanish players had been complaining about the organization surrounding the team, in particular the coach Jorge Vilda and his ally in the Spanish RFEF (the Spanish Football Federation, Real Federación Española de Fútbol) Luis Rubiales. The coach forbade players from locking their doors at night, when away at training camps, so that he could check up on them. In September 2022 fifteen players from the national team posted an open letter in which they requested that they no longer be called up to the squad. Despite this chaos, Spain deservedly won the World Cup. Some were hoping that they would not, in case a victory was exploited to vindicate Vilda's methods and Rubiales's leadership. However, what transpired had the dramatically opposite outcome.

With the world's media watching, Rubiales entered the pitch to celebrate with the team at the end of the game. However, this first involved him bizarrely carrying striker Athenea del Castillo over his shoulder: something he would clearly never have even attempted with a man. Holding her by the back of her thighs, it is hard not to see this as a symbolic sexist and patriarchal act. What did he mean by carrying her in this way? What signals did it send? That she was his trophy? Whatever his intentions, the images looked like masculine dominance asserted, with a corresponding loss of bodily autonomy of the athlete.

However, worse was to follow during the medal ceremony. Rubiales had been invited to join the dignitaries congratulating the teams and stood in a line-up next to Queen Letizia of Spain and her sixteen-year-old daughter Sofía. Overly and inappropriately affectionate as the Spanish players passed, when it was Jenni Hermoso's turn, Rubiales grabbed her head and kissed her on the lips, when she physically could not free herself. To cap it off, Rubiales was then filmed grabbing his own crotch when the trophy was presented and video also emerged of coach Vilda touching the breast of a member of staff while celebrating the game's only goal. There is no doubt that he touched her breast, the only possible question being whether or not it was intentional.

As with the Athenea del Castillo incident, these behaviours were indicative of a culture in which the men owned the women's bodies. They displayed their entitlement to the women: entitlements to kiss, to carry them away, to enter their bedrooms. Furthermore, the fact that they felt able to do this so openly, on live television, next to the Royal Family, showed the impunity they expected and had been able to assume, clearly for some time.

The surrender of bodily autonomy, as we have seen, is a prerequisite for women in sport, leaving women participants in sport all too vulnerable to abuse. We saw in Chapter Three one aspect of this surrender. Women have been obliged to prove their woman-hood as a precondition of their participation, including intimate and intrusive testing, in some cases genital inspection. Potential abusers have been able to make a connection here, however, since if women must give up their bodily autonomy, then it opens up the possibility of using those bodies for sexual harassment and abuse. One of the most infamous and disturbing cases in *Women's Sport* concerns Larry Nassar, who worked as the team doctor for the United States women's gymnastics national team, a position which he held for eighteen years. During that time, he sexually assaulted at least 265 young women, many of them child gymnasts, under the guise of medical treatment.

Larry Nassar was able to abuse his position because of the particularities of the sporting context. There are two factors that enable such abuse. First, the power dynamic: athletes are typically expected to obey the instructions of coaches and medical staff without question. If they want to reach the top, they are encouraged to do whatever it takes and whatever their coaching and medical staff tell them. If they do not, then they risk their place on the team, and by extension their career, livelihood and even personhood (for young elite athletes in this system, their sport is their whole self). Second, bodily surrender: since the body is the vehicle through which we perform our sporting feats, this lack of autonomy will potentially involve others having access to the athlete's body. If we put the power dynamic and bodily surrender together, we get an extremely dangerous situation in which sexual abuse is possible.

The fightback

Our aim is not to be a counsel of despair since we believe that there is more hope for the future of women and queer people in sport than there has ever been. The subsequent responses to the Larry Nassar case and, perhaps more significantly, the Luis Rubiales incident, show how the culture has changed. The Nassar case revealed the need for proper athlete protection and safeguarding, especially when children are involved but also for women generally. We should not ignore the men who have been sexually abused too: former coaches Barry Bennell and Bob Higgins both served prison sentences in the UK for sexually abusing young men in sport. Hopefully we learn from what has gone before.

However, these responses are inadequate on their own. They tend to be reactive, with new measures introduced in response to crimes that have already occurred instead of anticipating the systemic conditions that allow them to arise. Further, they are usually presented as 'bad apple' cases: these abusers are simply evil, unique individuals that we can do little to stop. Again, this does not challenge the system that produced them and very often protected them. Complaints were raised against Nassar from as early as 1997 but no action was taken against him until 2015. Nassar operated within a system of power that he knew would protect him and undermine complainants.

The response to the Rubiales case has gone beyond this, however. With so much now shared on social media, Jenni Hermoso was seen celebrating in the changing room after the game and, referring to Rubiales's actions, saying 'I really didn't like that.' As the story went viral, however, the RFEF put out a statement that seemingly included Hermoso's words:

It [the kiss] was a totally spontaneous mutual gesture due
to the immense joy of winning a World Cup. The president
and I have a great relationship, his behaviour towards all
of us has been outstanding and it was a natural gesture of
affection and gratitude. We can't think any more about a
gesture of friendship and gratitude, we won a World Cup
and we're not going to deviate from what's important.[10]

The problem was that Hermoso was not willing to go along
with this and made it clear, via the players' union, that she had
been placed under intense pressure to put her name to such a
statement. Indeed, this looked like a further abuse and a closing
of ranks by the institutional power around Rubiales. After the
story gained more and more attention, a press conference was
announced in which he was expected to resign but instead insisted
'I will not resign' five times.

What was encouraging, however, was that the athlete was
not willing to give up, in this instance, and was supported by an
international outcry. The entire Spanish team – now the World
Champions – insisted that they would not play another game
while Rubiales ran the RFEF. They were joined by some players
from the men's team, which also falls under the RFEF's authority.
Eleven of the women's coaching staff resigned. With the media
spotlight on the women's game like never before, this became an
opportunity for systemic change rather than a vindication of the
men in charge. It was notable how supportive the women's sporting community was. Even the defeated England team, far from
showing any resentment towards the winners, came out fully in
support of their fellow women athletes. The team captain, Leah
Williamson, put out a statement on behalf of all the Lionesses:

Unacceptable actions allowed to happen by a sexist and patriarchal organization. Abuse is abuse and we have all seen the truth. The behaviour of those who think they are invincible must not be tolerated and people shouldn't need convincing to take action against any form of harassment. We all stand with you, @jennihermoso and all players of the Spanish Team.[11]

The significance of this statement is hard to overestimate. It presents us with a whole sports team and its captain willing to invoke the notion of patriarchy: such a politically loaded term that shows acceptance of a deeper analysis than just one or two 'bad apples'. Patriarchy is a whole system of oppression. Indeed, the statement directly attributes patriarchy to the organization, and sexism too. They are saying not just that Rubiales and Vilda are sexist, but that the whole of the RFEF is systemically misogynist in covering for them. This concurs with philosopher Kate Manne's accounts of patriarchy, misogyny and sexism, which are not just about what is in an individual's thoughts and intentions but are also manifest in behaviours, organizations and policies.[12] It was clear that in the immediate aftermath of the World Cup, a propaganda machine had swung into action with the intention of preserving the established power and silencing the athletes. Vitally, and with the support of an athlete community, the players this time could not be silenced.

In the days that followed, with the RFEF still not backing down or taking any action at all, FIFA, the world governing body, stepped in and suspended Rubiales. The injustice of the matter was becoming so apparent that FIFA could not ignore the problem. The community had displayed unity, and they had taken public opinion with them. This public relations coup for the RFEF, of winning the World Cup, turned out to be their death knell. Vilda was sacked. Rubiales resigned. Women had used the power their sporting success had brought them to challenge an abusive system they had witnessed in operation.

As the Lionesses' statement recognizes, it is not simply individual men who are sexist or behave in patriarchal ways. Patriarchy is a system of power. We can think of it as an ideology: an idea that does harm primarily, though not exclusively, to women and queer people. The idea may work mainly through men though, again, not exclusively so. Women can themselves perpetrate patriarchy by endorsing a secondary and inferior role; indeed, in some cases, joining the argument for the alleged natural superiority of man, including the rigid enforcement of the gender binary and accompanying norms.

This is why it is important that we advocate for a feminist vision of sport, since it is a subversive act of defiance to challenge male dominance. Patriarchy would keep the sporting goods for the use of some to assert dominance and power over others, not just because they gain the benefit but also because it perpetuates the patriarchal myth of superiority. The acceptance that women (and queer people) can and must play sport is now widespread. They will no longer be denied. But the fight for equality is far from over. Patriarchy has one last rearguard action up its sleeve and it has proved very effective so far. This is the imposition and continued maintaining of a sexual segregation of sport, sold to women as being in their best interests but, as we will next argue in Chapter Five, is far from it.

Women and queer people have many reasons not to be happy with sport. They have endured various forms of informal and formal exclusions, and when they have participated, they have often been 'punished' for doing so, up to and including the suffering of sexual abuse. One response would be to opt out of what we know as sport altogether. We can indeed see lower participation rates for women, but this is no longer the trend. Another response is to limit one's activities to countercultural feminist sports. Despite this, sport, as an organized social practice in which we are encouraged to develop our physical capabilities to the best they can be, is overall a human good, to which all of us should have equal access. Excluding someone from sport harms them. Instead of accepting any form of exclusion, therefore, we encourage everyone to demand inclusion. As we will argue in our final two chapters, however, it is important that women's inclusion be on their own terms instead of the terms that patriarchy would impose. We will argue for *Feminist Sport.*

5

Beyond the Binary

There is sport, and there is sport played by women. It seems that we always have to specify when we are talking about *Women's Sport*, though we rarely bother to say *Men's* sport. That's just *Sport*. A look at the BBC football website in early 2024, for instance, found coverage of the World Cup – and the *Women's* World Cup. We even saw the absurdity, on the same website, of a league table that read Manchester City Women, Arsenal Women, Chelsea Women, and so on. It was a tiresome read. The other league table, by contrast, never says Manchester City *Men*. This is what Simone de Beauvoir meant when she wrote that women are always seen as the 'Other', while men are the default. So much of the othering occurs through the language we use.

The division of sport into men's and women's categories is seldom challenged. It just is. We assume it to be natural, necessary and sensible. A reflection of sexual division. And because of this, it is not even worth asking the question why this division exists in the first place. But as we've seen in previous chapters, far from being the reason that separate categories exist, sport creates sex differences. Similarly, biology, contrary to popular belief, doesn't simply reflect sex categories, but rather sex categories are created by biologists, who make a series of judgement calls and decisions to create a taxonomy that fits most of us into two categories. People themselves are not always so neatly divided into the two boxes of 'male' and 'female', however. Humans have always existed along a spectrum. We have deliberately avoided use of the terms 'male' and 'female' thus far in this book (other than when we've quoted), since they are often used in service of a view that we reject: that gender is reducible to biology. Society tends to use those terms when talking about animals. We might speak of male and female insects, lizards, snakes and rats: basically creatures that don't bear individual names. Humans are more than merely animals. They are conscious and social beings with individual names: much more than their biology. This is why we call them women rather than females. Again, language matters.

Patriarchy's preference is that sport should uphold specific White, cisgendered, heterosexual masculine (and, by contrast, feminine) ideals. To do so, sport must exclude women and anyone who doesn't conform to strict rules about what (White, cisgendered, heterosexual, masculine) men should be (except for Black men, whose role in sport becomes to further harmful racist stereotypes). But, given changes of attitudes in wider society, and the growing visibility and acceptance of not only women but gender expansive people (and marginalized people more generally too), this has proven unsustainable. It is too obviously exclusionary. Patriarchy's response, then, has been to allow (some) women's participation in sport but in a way that reinforces patriarchy; namely, by 'allowing' women to participate and compete but only under very strict conditions that reinforce the myth of masculine superiority and feminine inferiority, and therefore 'male' and 'female'.

In this chapter we set about challenging one of the most sacred orthodoxies of sport: that it should be divided into 'males' and 'females'. We do this by reversing the standard view on who benefits from the separation of sport into *Sport* and *Women's Sport*. The dominant view is that *Women's Sport* needs to be a 'protected' space (on the grounds of safety and fairness). Our key claim, however, is that *Women's Sport* is not simply separated from men's but, rather, is specifically *segregated*. On this account, segregation is a tool of patriarchal control.

Understanding *Women's Sport* through the lens of segregation allows us to further advance our argument about how this categorization works to uphold strong gendered and racialized hierarchies. As such, we want to outline a distinction between protected and segregated spaces and explain how and why *Women's Sport* is an example of the latter, rather than enacting the former. We also discuss the implications thereof. And we want to stress the difference between 'sex-based' rights and human rights.

Protection, 'sex-based' rights and human rights

In recent years, much has been made of *Women's Sport* as needing to be a so-called 'protected' space. The story goes that women need a separate category in sport (and, in the same vein, separate bathrooms and prisons) as a safeguarding measure. On this account, men, simply by virtue of being men, are stronger and more powerful but also more violent than women, and as such protected spaces provide women with safety to participate in public life. In sport, the argument goes, this protected space allows women opportunities to succeed, for without this protection from men no woman will ever be able to win again (or very few, anyway). This argument hinges on two underlying assumptions: 1) that men are and always will be stronger and more powerful than women; and 2) that without protection, women will be at risk of violence and/or harm. We have discussed this argument in part in Chapter Two, in terms of debunking the underlying assumptions.

A protected space in sport is meant to be for the benefit of those who are in that protected category. For example, in the UK, the Equality Act (2010) recognizes eight protected characteristics. It is deemed unlawful to discriminate against someone on the basis of these characteristics: because of their age, race, sex and so on. In terms of sex, this doesn't mean that only women are protected. That would make it a sex-based law, which is precisely what early feminists fought against. They fought for the radical notion that women should have the same rights and responsibilities as all others do on the basis that they are humans, rather than being othered and treated differently because they are women. Therefore, sport should be offered to all (including women, disabled people and young people, for example) on the basis that they are people who should be afforded the same opportunities as everyone else. In this way, protection in law provides equality.

This has been twisted in recent years to justify a re-emerging view that women need a protected category on the basis of being women, rather than simply human beings. This is what some are now calling 'sex-based rights'. This has set the scene for the argument that women need protection for 'fairness' and for their 'safety', which is often pitted against equality (or inclusion). On this account, fairness for women is compromised by equality because, if allowed to compete against women, men would dominate and women would rarely see success again. And equality compromises safety for women because men are always bigger and stronger, and this physical imbalance places women at risk in places where men and women mix. Worries about 'fairness' and 'safety', in this case, betray an underlying transphobic and misogynistic moral panic. These arguments about women needing protection through separation are deeply paternalistic. They rely on benevolent sexism, drawing on myths about women being the weaker and more vulnerable sex: what the early English feminist Mary Wollstonecraft called 'the insolent condescension of protectorship'.[1] They also do a disservice to men by binding them to toxic masculinity, not worthy of fairness or safety themselves. Sex essentialism is then reified by upholding old, outdated ideas about men's and women's bodies, masculine and feminine traits, and the sex binary.

If we move beyond the red herring that is the supposed friction between safety, fairness and equality/inclusion, we can open up new conversations about other, innovative ways of organizing sport (and society more broadly) that don't rely on sex/gender as a crude proxy for values that we may have, including fairness and safety. Indeed, this would also allow for more equitable inclusion for all as full human beings. For example, bio-banding (categorizing teenagers by growth and maturation, rather than age) has allowed us to look beyond age alone as a proxy for size and maturity level in teenagers (we all know that two fifteen-year-olds can be at vastly different stages of growth and maturity depending on the stage of puberty they are in). This is an innovative way of creating more appropriate categories that facilitate safety, fairness and inclusion that doesn't require those categories to start with dividing young people up into boys and girls. Some sports, including combat sports, separate participants primarily by skill level to ensure safe and appropriate matching up for training and competition. Karate has the coloured belt system. We may also think of the classification system in disability or Para sports, where athletes are classified according to their disability (though we recognize that this classification system and in particular the process of classification remains rather crude and is widely criticized). We can think of each of these categorizations as different approaches to providing protected spaces for the purposes of safe and fair and inclusive sport for all, opening up new possibilities for how we might think about sport and how it is structured in the future. This is called a human-rights framework, as opposed to a sex-based rights framework.[2]

While these approaches may take a little more time and effort to get right, they are in many instances far more appropriate than using sex alone as a proxy for safety and fairness (and focusing on safety and fairness as the only values we should foster in and through sport). In general, there is huge overlap between people: small, flexible men; big, powerful women; and every possible combination in between (for cis and trans and non-binary people alike). Sex is a crude tool if ultimately equity is our aim. Sex-based approaches are also at risk of being exploited by systems of oppression. If we are to move towards sport as a safe and fair space for all, we need to push back against twisted ideas about women needing protection to be granted by some benevolent men in power, and back to the idea that everyone, regardless of their gender, should not only be safe, but feel safe in our sporting spaces. Distorted, misogynistic ideas about protection for women are not about protection, but rather are closer to systems of segregation that we as a society have fought to outlaw. To use a protectionist framework to serve the majority at the expense of the minority (as calls to ban trans women from women's sport does) is to distort the purpose of human rights approaches.

Under a human rights framework, people are protected simply by virtue of being people. There is no hierarchy. According to the United Nations:

> The human rights-based approach (HRBA) is a conceptual framework for the process of human development that is normatively based on international human rights standards and operationally directed to promoting and protecting human rights. It seeks to analyse inequalities which lie at the heart of development problems and redress discriminatory practices and unjust distributions of power that impede development progress and often result in groups of people being left behind.[3]

Under this framework, we can see that there are good reasons why children's sports, for example, should operate within the protections this affords. We don't divide these protections into some for White children and others for Black children, or by Girl children and Boy children, but rather we recognize that *all* children must enjoy *all* their rights by virtue of being full human beings.

It is within this human rights framework that we think the sex division of sport should be understood and so, too, any claims about protected spaces. However, according to our account, *Women's Sport* is not a protected space after all but a segregated one. We must, therefore, turn to the distinction between protected and segregated spaces and make sure it is clearly established. This will allow us to support the claim that *Women's Sport* is specifically a segregated rather than protected space. There are at least two ways in which we can make the distinction between protected and segregated spaces: 1) on the basis of who benefits; and 2) on the basis of their entrance and exit conditions.

Who benefits?

A protected space in sport would be created for the benefit of those who are in the protected category. For example, in most sports we are reluctant to allow adults to compete against children, presumably because those children would face insurmountable disadvantages against an adult, as well as a host of other reasons. If a sport is organized into under-12, under-18 and under-21 categories, however, the children and youths involved can develop their sporting prowess alongside their peers. As mentioned above, other protected spaces, justifiable in a similar way, concern skill level and disability but in theory could be made on the basis of bio-banding or any other criterion that serves the best interests of those protected.

Many of our opponents will insist that *Women's Sport* operates in a similar protected category. Some of the arguments used will be that women need a protected space in which to play sport since, first, they would never win sporting encounters if they were competing against men, as men have such a natural physical advantage. By the same reasoning, it would be humiliating for women to compete against men since they would be so obviously outclassed and made to look hopeless. This is the fairness concern that was outlined above. So, too, can a safety concern be raised: namely, that women could be injured by men if they come into direct competition, especially in any contact sport. It is not merely concerns about injury that are raised as safety issues. There can also be suggestions of the possibility of abuse, including sexual abuse, as outlined in our previous chapter, if men and women compete together. There are other contexts where women-only spaces are preferred and sport, by virtue of its emphasis on physicality, is often brought into the discussion. However, we think that all of these reasons are spurious, as we will go on to detail, and that *Women's Sport* exists in a segregated space rather than a protected one.

A segregated space, by contrast, does not exist for the benefit or protection of those who are within it; rather, it benefits the system of power at play. A stronger way of putting this is to say that segregation is a tool employed for the benefit of the oppressor, whereas a protected space (under a human rights framework) operates (at least in an ideal world) for the benefit of the oppressed. In a patriarchal world, and given what we have previously discussed about *Women's Sport* being created as a tool of oppression, we feel that this analysis of *Women's Sport* being a segregated space is a compelling one. The language and mechanism of oppression is apt too when drawing on historical examples of segregation, the most notorious of which is racialized segregation such as that operated in the twentieth century in the south of the United States and in apartheid South Africa. There, we know, the system of oppression implemented segregation as a form of control over Black people and People of Colour so as to uphold a patriarchal White supremacist system of power. We don't think it is hyperbole to say that segregating women who play sport into a category of their own – *Women's Sport* – and then policing that category violently, is an example of the use of the same method of oppression by the very same system of power.

Further, once the mechanisms of oppression are in place, they become part of the justification for that oppression. White people deserve the best education because they are higher achieving, for a perverted example, yet one used before, in segregationist America, and still used by racists today. Rather than recognizing that it is the opportunity and resources that White people receive (and, by contrast, the extreme lack of opportunity and resources Black people receive) that creates the higher achievement, intellect is positioned as innate to White people, and Black people are discriminated against on the basis that they simply don't have it. In this way, racialized difference and hierarchy is first created and then justified through segregation. Similarly, rather than recognizing that it is opportunity and resources that create higher achievement in sport for men, sporting ability is positioned as innate to men and women are discriminated against on the basis that they simply aren't as good. Gendered hierarchy, rather than reflecting inequality and being an answer to it, first creates and then justifies inequality through the segregated space that is *Women's Sport*.

Entrance and exit

Now we can outline a more rigorous and conceptual way of distinguishing protection from segregation since this will not only add to the case for them being distinct but will also be a basis for our interpretation of *Women's Sport* as being segregated rather than protected.

The idea here is that we can distinguish two or more systems on the basis of their consequences. Someone might think of protected and segregated spaces as amounting to pretty much the same thing, but we can prove this wrong if we show that one of them has a consequence that the other does not. Let us make this concrete, then, and explain how protection and segregation differ in this respect.

It is important for a protected space that there is no voluntary entrance into it. One cannot simply elect to enter the space but must, in the relevant sense, qualify for it. An adult will not be allowed to play against children, for instance. One qualifies for the protected category by virtue of meeting certain criteria, such as being under a specified age. However, there may be voluntary exit from protected spaces. Suppose a child participating in youth sports is clearly good enough to compete in an open-aged competition. Then, unless there are rules preventing this, they are allowed to do so with fully informed consent. Indeed, there are numerous instances of athletes who could continue to compete in youth sports, yet nevertheless compete in elite sports.

What distinguishes a segregated space from a protected space is that, while they are the same in respect of having no voluntary entry, unlike a protected space, a segregated space has no voluntary exit either. We call this the no-voluntary-exit criterion for the distinctness of segregation.

Let us consider the classic case of segregation again, that of racial segregation in twentieth-century United States. It was clear that no one was permitted to exit the segregated space. African American people could not choose to sit in the bus seats reserved for White people, or choose to go to schools from which they were excluded by virtue of being Black. If they did sit in the reserved seats, as in Rosa Parks's famous protest, harsh consequences applied. They could not opt out of enslavement either. Similarly in apartheid South Africa, Black people were not allowed to participate with or compete against White people in sport. Segregated sport spaces for Black people were not a choice, but rather an imposition that was policed violently. This segregation was enacted on the justification that White people (and particularly White women and children) needed to be protected from Black people (Black men in particular), on the (incorrect) basis that Black people are dangerous and barely human. Violation of the no-voluntary-exit principle is therefore met with significant penalty in order to uphold the status quo, and is based on extreme social discrimination.

This establishes that protected and segregated spaces differ since they have different features or consequences. There is the possibility of voluntary exit from a protected space but there is no possibility of voluntary exit from a segregated space. We can now add this to the claim that a segregated space exists in the interests of those in power, whereas a protected space exists in the interests of the oppressed. Note that these two ways of distinguishing protected and segregated spaces are independent of each other. They raise separate considerations: one about the natures of segregation and protection and the other about the justice or injustice of them being implemented. However, these two considerations are not entirely unconnected. A specifically segregated space, rather than a protected space, is purposefully created and violently upheld by systems of oppression because it allows no voluntary exit. The oppressor cannot allow the oppressed to up and leave their oppression. The whole point of no-voluntary-exit is so that the segregation can uphold a system of power.

Which is *Women's Sport*?

With the distinction now clear, we can return to the question of whether *Women's Sport* exists as a protected or a segregated space. Let us apply what we have learnt. First, is voluntary exit possible from *Women's Sport*? Are women allowed to opt out of their category to compete in the men's? In practice, women cannot. Historically, we have seen the occasional feminist killjoy (in Chapter Two) competing against men prior to the creation of the *Women's Sport* category; or, as in the case of Bobbi Gibb, when it was simply assumed that no woman would attempt to compete. But, once *Women's Sport* is created, voluntary exit is barred no matter how good a woman is. When Lindsey Vonn, an American alpine ski racer, expressed her wish to compete with men in the 2012–13 season, after proving herself one of the greatest ski racers – men or women – of all time, she was unable to persuade the International Ski Federation to let her do so. Years later she reflected on this frustration in an interview with Euronews, stating: 'It wasn't men against women, it was just men were better and I wanted to race against the best . . . I wanted to improve myself.'[4] But she could not. In a patriarchal world, women *must* remain in *Women's Sport*.

As we outlined in Chapters Two and Three, there is a historical pattern of women being violently prevented from competing against men, *especially* if there is a danger that they they could do so successfully. Formal exclusion may previously have been considered unnecessary, since women would not compete with and challenge men, but as soon as they do so, we have seen, then the barrier is put in place. Why might that be? Does *Women's Sport* exist in the interest of the oppressor? This is indeed the verdict we should give. We have seen that (men's) *Sport* attracts vastly more resourcing and funding. It would be reasonable for women athletes to want access to that. Suppose a woman footballer wanted to play in the men's game because the salaries there are much higher, the training facilities are better, the status is greater, the competition is stronger and so on. She is simply not allowed to do so, even if she is good enough. Some readers might be sceptical that a woman would ever be good enough to compete against men. But this is where we want to flip the script and return to the point that the segregated space of *Women's Sport* exists in the interest of patriarchal systems of oppression and helps create, rather than responds to, the athletic differences between women and men.

Advantaging the already advantaged

Of course, systems of power use any means at their disposal to deflect from, and deny, the privilege they create and uphold. Naturalizing ideas about superiority is one such tool, as we have shown. Conceptions of both sex/gender and race essentialism are key. And, at the same time, the ways in which structural sexism and racism (among others, including ableism, classism and so on) work to produce and compound inequality are played down or ignored.

This helps set up a system in which society can be defeatist about marginalization (women are simply not as good at sport as men) while at the same time blaming marginalized people for their own inferiority (as Gianni Infantino did in 2023, telling women footballers that they should simply work harder to 'convince us men what we have to do'). They might even claim that they, the 'more naturally gifted' group, would themselves be oppressed without segregation. And there are, of course, men who think of themselves as oppressed simply when their own structural privilege is pointed out to them. Indeed, to quote the adage (of unknown origin) 'when you're accustomed to privilege, equality feels like oppression.'

This used to be said about women's brains too. The idea of 'pink brains' and 'blue brains' (women's smaller, more fragile and emotional brains, and men's bigger, more robust and rational brains) was for a very long time a useful story that locked women out of education and many professions. And while that myth and method of patriarchal control has largely been debunked, the impression of women's supposedly innate physical inferiority endures – locking women out of their own flourishing.

The inferiority myth is one story. And although it is the narrative favoured by the forces of patriarchy, is it also attractive to some women (for women can and sometimes do uphold patriarchy too). These women, including some who position themselves as feminists, are swayed by the point that, because men are the main perpetrators of violence against women, that violence itself is held within the penis (or, to be more specific, the XY chromosomes). This makes the idea of women-only spaces and sex-based rights seem attractive. But this kind of sex essentialism harms men and women (and everyone beyond that binary too), by labelling all men as violent and all women as helpless. It fails to recognize that women can be and are violent too, including against men and children. That violence is not a genetic trait, but rather a social one.

While one can hardly blame women for wanting to take steps against the very real problem of men's violence against women, and we agree this is important and valuable work, doing so by using sex as a proxy for violence neglects to take into account the full scope of how and why violence is perpetrated. The protectionist response, which takes the form of advocating for women-only spaces as the primary solution to the problem (which, under this framework, can only be *men's* violence, for women's violence is ignored and erased completely), is too crude to meet its aims. Violence against women isn't simply because of (their) sex; it is about power. This is because the protectionist response has one major problem: it fails to challenge the patriarchal system that creates the oppression in the first place. It attempts a defensive action against a symptom of patriarchy but does nothing to challenge patriarchy itself. Indeed, since it accepts the same narrative that patriarchy promotes – that men are physically superior and naturally prone to violence and that women are relatively fragile and open to exploitation – these two opposed sides are brought together in an uncomfortable and unexpected alliance. Once again, it provides useful insight here to compare this with how Black men in particular are harmed by race essentialism (the story goes that Black men are abnormally big and strong and violent, and by contrast White women are exceptionally small and fragile and at risk), and by policies and laws that have been created around this discrimination both in the past and today.

We must resist and dismantle White supremacist patriarchy and the narratives that serve it. A big part of our work in this book is to provide the tools by which to do so, through some old-fashioned consciousness-raising. As a society, it is important to recognize that patriarchy harms boys and men too, through toxic expectations of and ideas about manhood and masculinity. Boys and men, far from being naturally violent or strong or smart, are taught how to be these things. And this is reinforced with every step of their lives. Any boy or man who does not conform is punished violently too. Hence, patriarchy constructs not only fragile femininity but toxic masculinity. Following Manne's analysis in *Down Girl: The Logic of Misogyny*, we see misogyny as the policing arm of patriarchy. It enforces a binary of two distinct sets of gender roles and norms, and patrols the boundary between them, sanctioning anyone who attempts to reject those norms, cross over to the other side or refuse to pick a side.

Feminist values

Let us then consider a different narrative: a feminist one. The arrangements, structures and organizations of sport developed within a patriarchal world also uphold patriarchal control. *Sport* was neither designed nor intended for equality. Its major purpose is not to break down systems of oppression, but to uphold them. In this way, *Sport* (and, by way of contrast, *Women's Sport*) exists to valorize those at the top of the patriarchal hierarchy. Anyone who does not fit the mould (including men who reject toxic masculinity, women and queer people) thus becomes the Other, and their existence then becomes the justification for oppression.

But patriarchy is, as Angela Saini says in her 2023 book *The Patriarchs*, itself fragile. Once put in place, it does not endure for evermore. It has to be repeatedly maintained and the differences between men and women constantly recreated, lest they be shown to be what they really are: a cover. *Women's Sport* was created as a segregated space so that, in stark contrast with the specimens on display in *Sport*, these categories would provide prime examples of what it means to be a 'real' man or woman. Breaking down the boundaries between these two categories, and indeed between men and women themselves more broadly, creates an existential crisis. If there are no 'men' and no 'women' at all, how would society function? It feels, to the uninitiated, like a disaster waiting to happen.

But it doesn't need to be the catastrophe that we were taught to fear. As we have seen, difference – whether physical, mental, gendered, racialized – rather than being natural, is actually socially created. Differences are the outcome of processes and tools and mechanisms that are at play in the world whether we are aware of them or not. And every one of us, willingly or unwillingly, knowingly or unknowingly, plays a role in oiling these mechanisms and keeping these tools and processes in play.

Segregation in sport is a vital way in which the myth of male physical superiority is maintained since, like all segregation, it creates circumstances in which the best advantages and opportunities can be made inaccessible to the Other. The reason there is no voluntary exit from women's sport into men's is so that women cannot access the same advantages that men have. Feminists should not accept that biology is (sporting) destiny. There is nothing natural about men beating women in sports, being bigger, faster and stronger. Those differences are constructed. Indeed, part of what it is to become woman, in the aforementioned sense articulated by Beauvoir ('One is not born, but rather becomes, woman'), is to be forced to conform to fragility, be slower, be smaller, be softer and be weaker. Understanding and accepting the unpleasant truth that sport has been segregated into two distinct categories for these patriarchal purposes must be our starting point. If one instead acquiesces in the protectionist narrative, entering into the uncomfortable alliance with patriarchy, one will eventually realize, to invoke Audre Lorde, that the master's tools will never dismantle the master's house.[5]

Would men like it?

The argument so far has been that the sex-segregation of sport harms women by giving them fewer opportunities to flourish and thereby constructs their physical weaknesses compared to men. Some might still be sceptical. Our patriarchal conditioning is so strong that we may still claim that men's advantages are natural and that women should have to play their own sports so that they have a chance of winning. Here is another kind of argument, though. Would men themselves like it if it happened to them? Would they accept participation in a lesser version of sport?

We strongly suspect not, but one might ask how we could justify this verdict, given that men are currently performing better than women. Nevertheless, men do sometimes belong to groups that are not performing relatively well and we can see that, despite being in that situation, there has been no attempt to create a protected (segregated) space for them. Nor do we think there would be any willingness to accept the protected space if it were offered to them. And nor do we think it would be right to offer them a protected space on this basis either.

We offer two examples. The first concerns the men's 100 metres event at the Olympics. Over the last forty years, there have been eighty men's Olympic finalists and none have been White men. Now suppose someone were to offer the following proposal. White men do not seem to be competitive in this event. White men now don't ever even reach the final. Let's create a separate 100 metres for White men, to give them a chance of winning. They could at least enjoy a contest where they have a chance of success. This has not been proposed for the Olympics, thankfully, and sports have only been racially segregated in places that have had racial segregation under systems of oppression. But, on the same argument that we hear for *Women's Sport*, why would it not be acceptable? We can imagine reasons such as the following: such an arrangement would be demeaning, humiliating and patronizing. White men athletes prefer to compete against the best, no matter who they are, even if it means losing. These reasons are sound.

Nevertheless, the undoubted rejection of any such offer to give these White men a chance of winning their own event is quite revealing. It betrays the assumptions of supremacism that are an ideological ground for segregation. Granting women an apparently protected space is 'justified' by the tacit assumption that men are superior to women. Men are content to have separate sports since it supports their view of male supremacism. But this is why White men would never accept a protected space in sport, since it would be to concede a Black supremacism that they could never countenance, even if it were limited to just one event in one sport. We can add to this view an argument that it is wrong to separate people according to their race (for a great many reasons, including that race itself is also socially constructed), and treat them differently, but we note that sporting organizations are perfectly content to separate people according to their sex. Through this example we can see that sex, like race, is a social phenomenon and that the practical meaning of this construction can and does change over time.

The second example concerns marginalized nations in sport. Suppose a number of so-called 'developing' countries were identified that had performed badly in Olympic medal tables over the years. We may understand that in reality they have been economically exploited by colonialism, and so have been less able to invest heavily in sports infrastructure. Now, what would we make of a proposal that they should no longer be allowed to compete in the 'real' Olympics, since they have so little chance of winning, and instead will have their own version, the 'development Olympics', so that they might enjoy some success within their own developing-nation class? However, they could never be promoted to the proper Olympics, no matter how well they performed. They must forever remain in their protected category, for their own good. Again, it seems that no nation would want to take up this offer, much less be forced into it, especially if the funding, prize money and prestige was a small fraction of that of the real Olympic Games. No one wants to be secondary or unimportant. We all want a chance to participate and compete with the best; or at least to know that if we progress sufficiently we could qualify to compete against them. There might be years or decades of defeat along the way, but how can we improve unless we play against better athletes and sometimes, or always, lose?

The question, now, is that if in these examples it is wrong to have separate sports, why wouldn't we apply exactly the same reasoning to reject the separateness of women from *Sport*? Why oblige women (or anyone, for that matter) to accept a secondary and inferior form of the game? We cannot see a justification for it in this case if it doesn't exist in the other examples above. And if one doesn't apply the same reasoning, we can only think that an ideology of patriarchy is the basis.

If protection was the aim, we would not do it this way

Suppose someone were unmoved by these kinds of considerations and insisted that the protection of the athlete was the primary concern. Segregation, they might say, is better than nothing since it protects the women athletes, even if it does so with some cost to their freedom. Nevertheless, we can deny the force of this view by countering that if athlete protection really was the concern, we wouldn't do it this way. Simply dividing competitors into men and women does not, on its own, protect women, since sex as such isn't the relevant risk factor, and separation by sex would always need to be supplemented with genuine protections. This could be taken as a further argument against the interpretation that *Women's Sport* operates in a protected space and adds further credibility to the interpretation of segregation.

Suppose we accepted that in certain sports a difference in some physical attribute, such as weight, height or strength, could either endanger an opponent or give an unfair advantage such that it wouldn't be a worthy contest. These seem to be the main reasons offered in favour of setting up *Women's Sport* within a protected space since the additional fact can be invoked that currently, on average, men weigh more than women, are taller than women, stronger, and so on. Therefore, it is concluded, it can be dangerous and unfair to women to expect, or even allow, them to compete against men.

There are, however, many flaws to this argument. If a weight disparity matters in a sport, such as in rugby, then it does not justify separated events for men and women, even if weight or power disparities are dangerous and unfair. If they indeed are dangerous and unfair, then they are so regardless of the gender of the competitors. We allow adult rugby opponents to have any degree of weight or power differential as long as they are of the same gender. Why, then, is it suddenly dangerous and unfair only when it concerns people of different sexes? Why isn't exactly the same weight or power differential considered dangerous and unfair when opponents have the same sex? If we truly thought weight or power was a relevant factor in safety and fair competition, surely our protected spaces should be arranged around that instead of something that only very roughly maps on to it. Men may well be taller than women on average, but this does not mean that every man is taller than every woman; far from it. It also ignores the diversity of gender expansive people. This is the problem of taking sex as a proxy for the supposed characteristics that could endanger or disadvantage an athlete: they are not found all and exclusively in the notion of the opposite sex. Differentials in factors such as weight and power are to be found within humans, regardless of sex classification, and equality in those same factors can be found among people of a different sex. In fact, we argue that using sex as a crude proxy is, in fact, negligent. We can only conclude that the athlete-protection credentials of sex-separation are spurious.

Regarding fairness, rather than safety, we see that for similar reasons the arguments from differences fail. It is never considered problematic within (men's) *Sport* when one opponent is vastly more physically endowed than the others, such as Michael Phelps was in swimming or Jonah Lomu in rugby. Those athletes could completely destroy their opponents, in a sporting sense, and became dominating winners. In these cases, however, their extraordinary physical advantages were seen as a gift and something their rivals simply had to deal with. Within *Women's Sport*, where a competitor is conspicuously better endowed physically than her rivals, this is instead viewed suspiciously, including cases where the athlete's gender is brought into question, as we saw in Chapter Three. Dominance within one's sex category is celebrated for men's *Sport*, suspicious for women's. Doubly so for

Black women, Women of Colour and gender expansive people in *Women's Sport*. A rejoinder could be that exactly the same reasoning occurs in other protected spaces. Perhaps what justifies age categories is that, on average, junior athletes will be smaller and less capable than fully grown adults. If one can take age as a proxy for physical stature, why not take sex? As reasoned above, however, we are already moving beyond age categories because we know they don't work for what we want them to do. Where we do still use age categories, we permit the possibility of voluntary exit. Hence, if a youth competitor was big enough, strong enough, mentally mature enough and capable enough, we allow the possibility of them competing in an older age category or even the open-age category. Indeed, Jonah Lomu played for the full New Zealand side when he had only just turned nineteen years old and still qualified to play at under-21 level. Junior sports are not designed as a cage in which to trap young people. They are designed to assist their sporting development, which can be benefited by being alongside peers who are going through similar processes of maturation, but sometimes there are also benefits in playing against older athletes. That is not a consideration in sex-segregated sports where adult athletes are obliged to accept peers only of the same sex.

We can see, therefore, that sex-separation fails to protect athletes in some of the ways used to justify its imposition. There is nothing to stop a woman rugby player facing a far heavier and stronger opponent of the same sex. Or a far more skilled one. Protection would only come through further, actual protections, such as weight or skill categorization, or indeed high-quality training and skills development. The fact that the separation of men's and women's sports fails to provide such protections, and further neglects to provide women with the commensurate training and resources, only adds to the plausibility of *Women's Sport* existing in a segregated space rather than a protected one.

The protection of patriarchy

We have said that segregated spaces exist in the interest of systems of oppression. In the case of sport, one way in which sex-segregation serves the interest of the oppressor is in reserving all the best resources, facilities and incentives for men's *Sport*, thus assisting them to develop greater athleticism than those who are relegated to *Women's Sport*. But there is an overarching purpose that sex-segregation serves for the oppressor, which is to protect patriarchy. Patriarchy is thereby revealed as more fragile than it presents itself to be (in this respect, men's sport operates in a protected space more so than women's). Let us consider this point, put forward by Angela Saini, more closely.[6]

Suppose men's physical supremacy were perfectly 'natural' in the sense that it sprang necessarily from the biological differences between men and women. If that were so, men wouldn't need to preserve for themselves the best opportunities and resources for their physical training. There would be no need to make women relatively disadvantaged, compared to men, in such a thorough, systematic and sustained way as has been enacted historically. The fact that women have been persistently disadvantaged shows that the physical dominance of men over women has to be constantly recreated and sustained throughout time. This physical dominance is clearly a delicate thing since patriarchy dare not let women benefit from the same conditions that men do in sport. Men's advantage cannot be relied upon to persist unaided. The social and organizational arrangements put in place by men clearly have an effect of maintaining rather than challenging the differences between the sexes, which is another way of saying that those differences are socially constructed.

The fragility of patriarchy is revealed in another way too. As well as denying women the same competitive conditions as men, sex-segregation also renders direct comparisons between men and women difficult, if not impossible. What fragile patriarchy especially cannot permit is the possibility of a woman looking better than a man, by beating him in direct competition. This is betrayed in the responses to the occasions when it has actually happened, such as Zhang Shan's Olympic Gold in 1992. Let us remind ourselves. The event was mixed-sex at the time, since in shooting competitions it is hard to identify any remotely plausible rationale for sex-segregation on the grounds of either fairness or athlete safety. After Zhang's victory, women were banned from competing by the International Shooting Union and were unable to compete at the next Olympics, in 1996. At the Games after that, in 2000, women could compete but only in a women's version of the event. There are plenty of other similar cases too, as we have detailed in Chapter Two. We are certainly not saying that women would always beat men, if they competed together. Indeed, under current circumstances, this would be surprising. But the response of the sporting authorities in the instances where it has happened is revealing. It is a reaction of exclusion and segregation.

Against segregation

It is important to recognize and establish that *Women's Sport* is founded on segregation rather than protection since, rightly, protection is usually considered a good thing and segregation is usually considered a bad thing. And yet, as we have shown, it can be easy to mistake one for the other, or to pervert one in service of the other. Even those competing might believe that they do so within a protected rather than segregated space. Nevertheless, as we understand it, this is a significant mistake to make: tantamount, as the philosopher Rousseau once said, to rushing headlong to one's chains in the hope of gaining liberty.[7] Wollstonecraft took up this metaphor, and applied it specifically to women: 'is it surprising that some of them hug their chains.'[8] We reject racial segregation, for instance, and the segregation of women in many other domains. Women now compete against men for jobs, take the same university exams as men, stand for election against men, and so on. And further, so do trans and non-binary and queer and gender expansive people.

What seems particularly conspicuous about the case of sport, however, is a reluctance and even refusal to first allow that women ought to be the *physical* equals of men, and second to move beyond the binary. As we said in Chapter Two, sport is a feminist issue. Does this mean, then, that we advocate the immediate sex desegregation of sport? And what would be the consequences of doing that?

The simple answer to this question for us is that, yes, sport should be desegregated. The deeper answer is that this should itself occur within a broader dismantling of gender inequality and patriarchal power structures. There are many factors that explain men's relative better performances in sports than women's: men have always been praised for being big, encouraged to eat well and expected to take physically active roles, while women have been praised for being petite, admonished for having a healthy appetite and expected to take caring and domestic roles. This history of different expectations, which has aided a physical divergence between men and women, cannot be reversed overnight. Even if we look just at the current generation, there is still ample evidence of a whole gendered upbringing to consider. And yet, things are changing. Over the last one hundred years we have seen women's expansiveness grow exponentially, in all aspects including physicality, and now we are starting to see more visibly that of queer people too.

What a desegregation of sport would do, then, would be to remove not only the formal constraints on equal participation. It would create the possibility that we access the same facilities, resources and rewards. It would allow for the possibility of equal play conditions. No longer would some tennis players have only three sets while others get five, or some skiers be confined to the less-challenging downhill ski slope. Desegregating sport alone would not dismantle all the other, informal pressures on some people to be less physical than others, but it would make a contribution even there. As we explained in Chapter Four, sport plays an important role in how we understand ourselves as physical beings. If we see more people thriving, no matter their gender, this assists in the perception of equality and thereby aids everyone's liberation. Sport has a crucial role to play in changing wider attitudes and setting new expectations and ambitions.

Ideally, patriarchy should be dismantled entirely at the same time that sport is desegregated. We cannot, however, offer huge optimism that it will be. Suppose, then, that we have to address this issue in sub-optimal conditions. If we desegregate sport overnight but change little else about our world and about ourselves, we know that some historically marginalized people will have an initial disadvantage. Over time, with equal access to sport, we hope that such disadvantages would be lessened. But we can also look to other cases of desegregation and see what lessons to take from them.

Racial desegregation is accepted as the right thing to do even if it does not restore equality overnight. In South Africa, for instance, formal segregation has ended but it is still a reality informally since it remains true that White South Africans are intergenerationally wealthier than Black South Africans. What there should be is a recognition that one group has been historically disadvantaged and there is a case for restorative justice. In the instance of sport, some such principle should also apply. Having suffered countless historical injustices, disincentives and even bans, women and queer people should be assisted in their task of catching up with men, rather than being left to do it on their own as if there were no historical context for their current position. This project would be a matter of restorative justice – restoring what has been taken away – which is itself a complicated issue. How best this should be implemented is likely to vary from sport to sport and best managed by sporting bodies that have been purged of patriarchal dominance. But we will add some further thoughts of our own in the next chapter.

Let us take stock as we have covered a lot of ground in this chapter and seen some challenging ideas advanced. Sporting competitors are often divided into different categories. Sometimes this is for the athlete's own benefit and care, as in the case of protected characteristics. Sport can occur within a protected space, in these instances. *Women's Sport* is divided from men's but, we argue, this does not serve the interests of women but of patriarchy. Consequently, we understand *Women's Sport* to be confined to a segregated rather than protected space. Since there is no voluntary exit from this space, it becomes a cage in which women are captured, constrained and controlled. Like other forms of segregation, this constitutes an injustice. It is a manifestation of patriarchal power, with its justificatory wing of sexism and its policing wing of misogyny, keeping women in their purported place. And sport is a very important instance since it can be used to perpetuate the myth than men are naturally superior physically and hold their dominant place inevitably. The constant need to sustain and police segregation gives the lie to this interpretation, however. Patriarchy is fragile. Men need ongoing advantages to maintain their athletic superiority. Ideally, sex-segregation in sport would be abolished so that women and queer people can develop their athleticism in equal conditions to men. We note, however, that there are wider patriarchal structures to be dismantled so that everyone can have an equal chance. Among those, we should consider a vision of what sport should be. Can we offer a feminist vision of sport or are we advocating that sport for women should become exactly like men's? It is this topic to which we next turn.

6

The Future of Feminist Sport

Following the England Lionesses' victory in the Euro championship in 2022, *Women's Football* became hugely popular in that country. Subsequent Lionesses games sold out quickly, even when played at the huge 90,000-capacity Wembley Stadium. Domestic competitions also saw an uptake in season ticket sales: in the hundreds of per cent. This renewed interest did not seem confined to England, which had in some ways lagged behind other countries such as Germany and Sweden. A year later, the World Cup was held in Aotearoa New Zealand and Australia with unprecedented levels of support, even compared to the previous tournament in France four years prior. Stadiums were routinely sold out and the host nations were for a while taken over by the sport. Spectators who had bought tickets for (men's) Australian Rules Football games were filmed in the concourses during games watching screenings of the Matildas' quarter-final instead. Aotearoa New Zealand and Australia were seeing their own revolution.

There was a lot that seemed right about the 'women's game', which many commentators saw as better than the 'regular football'. It might be claimed that football played by men was faster, with a higher skill level, but this assumption was routinely being challenged. Football played by women also seemed to be contested in a manner closer to the spirit of the game, with little simulation, cheating or dissent being shown to the referee. But this didn't mean that it lost any of its excitement. One big reason why fans started watching women play football was the overall better spectator experience. The games were watched in a much friendlier atmosphere, with fans wanting *Women's Football* itself to succeed. There was less aggressive masculinity on show, and spectator violence, as far as we know, was non-existent. Women were enthused, certainly, but it was not only women. Men were there too, particularly men who had been put off by the toxic masculine culture of (men's) *Football*. The crowds drew many more families and children to see the games in person. For the first time, it seemed, young children of all genders would name women as their favourite footballers: not just their favourite *woman* footballer, but favourite footballer, period. DJs would be brought out before games and at half time, turning the night into a big party (mainly for the kids, who loved it). Dancing in the stands at half time has seldom occurred at *Football*. In *Women's Football*, it was the norm. There was also far greater LGBTQ+ visibility than at the men's, which is still regarded as not generally welcoming for the queer community, despite the notable efforts of some trailblazing supporter groups. There are plausible reasons for these differences in attitudes between the two sets of sports fans, to which we will come. However, these differences, and perceived superiority (at least in these regards) of the *Women's Sport* experience over the men's, presents us with an interesting question.

Women's Sport is seen as welcoming, safe, family friendly, LGBTQ+ friendly, kinder, more compassionate. On the other hand, *Sport* takes a win-at-all-costs approach. *Sport* has developed into a space where cheating, heckling, betting, hostility and even violence are par for the course. Much of the history of *Women's Sport* has shown a pattern of exclusion and a fight for the right to play. Women have fought for equal treatment: to be allowed to participate in the same sports and under the same conditions that men have always had. We have seen *Women's Sport* develop and, in some cases, flourish not because of the support it has received, but rather despite all the barriers that had to be overcome (and continue to plague it). This raises the question, though, of whether *Women's Sport* should continue the aim of becoming just like men's *Sport*. Is that the ultimate goal or end point of this process of development? Would women feel they had succeeded in sporting acceptance if their sports were indistinguishable from the men's in every way (except, of course, for the continued existence of sex-based categories)? Or, rather, should women instead aim to preserve what is currently distinctive and 'better' about *Women's Sport*? We are bound to wonder what the future of *Women's Sport* will look like and, more importantly, what it ought to look like.

From this position, the question then often posed is: do we want *Women's Sport* to become more like *Sport*, or do we want *Sport* to become more like *Women's Sport*?

Nurturing versus masculinity

There is a widespread understanding that toxic masculinity has corrupted men's *Sport*. There is more to this than homophobia alone. Indeed, we find quite a broad impact of this oppressive form of masculinity and a close connection to the patriarchy which it serves. Toxic masculinity shows how patriarchy, including the strict gender divide applied to sport, harms all of us, not just women.

Toxic masculinity means that you are not supposed to admit your vulnerabilities, or your feelings, or ask for help. You are supposed to be hard on others and on yourself. You will be ruthless against your rivals and give them no comfort when you inflict upon them their defeats. In turn, you expect no comfort when they defeat you. The victory is all that matters, and it is all or nothing: glory for the winners, shame for the losers. Indeed, the shame of defeat is considered a necessity, since only if it really hurts is one able to toughen up and do all in one's power to avoid this pain in the future. A sporting contest is like a war, and military metaphors abound. It's not a game but a battle, where some players are praised for being generals and the goal is to rout the opposition. Ruthlessness in men's *Sport* is accepted, indeed promoted, with its win-at-all-costs mindset. The idea that one would encourage an opponent to perform to their best, nurture them, be pleased for their victories, even over yourself, is complete anathema. There may, of course, be some variation among different men's sports, showing that such toxicity can come in degrees. Cricketers, for instance, may think of themselves as following a more moderate ethos, which does include greater care for others. Originating as a sport for *gentle*men, cricket saw itself as a cut above: destroy your opponents, but be polite as you do it.

This exposes the opportunity for a new vision for sport to be transformative for boys and men too. We are slowly starting to see some degree of acceptance of LGBTQ+ visibility in men's *Sport*. There are some Rainbow supporter groups forming for men's teams, and sports clubs that display Pride colours and flags or athletes who wear rainbow laces in their boots. But this is still far from fully achieved. Recent years have seen once again a rise in open homophobia and, inevitably not long after, transphobia and racism. We have seen players who had previously been diversity champions sell their principles for lucrative playing contracts in Saudi Arabia and other countries where there are fewer LGBTQ+ rights and rights for women.

It is hard to doubt that there are many gay athletes playing *Sport* who feel that they cannot publicly come out. For every Tom Daley, there will be any number who keep their orientation a secret, since playing sport without harassment means hiding their true selves. The problem is that patriarchy inflicts rigid binary gender norms on everyone. There are men who are expected to play this tough, masculine role who do not feel that it comes to them naturally. There is pressure on all of us, including men, who might feel obliged to laugh at homophobic remarks in the changing room while knowing that they would always prefer diversity. The gender norms – a slew of gender-based expectations – constrain us all. They tell us how we should be, and specifically that we have to fall into one of two groups and conform to the expectations of the group we are given.

In many ways, the current discussion matches, for the case of *Women's Sport*, what feminists have discussed in relation to women and men generally. Is there a distinctive set of 'feminine' and 'masculine' 'virtues' and, if women are to gain equality with men (for this case sits firmly within the binary structure), do they want to preserve or replace their assigned 'virtues'? This question is prominent in Mary Wollstonecraft's *A Vindication of the Rights of Woman* (1792), for instance.[1]

Let us take *caring* as an example of an alleged feminine virtue. There seems to be a view in the received understanding that women are, and ought to be, more caring than men. Women, by nature of being capable of becoming mothers, are, on this account, innately the more nurturing sex. Of course, men are capable of caring for others too, but the popular suggestion is that this trait is to be found more in women than in men, for evolutionary reasons. Men perhaps have other strengths instead.

There is a dilemma for feminist thinkers, however. Caring seems to be a positive virtue. Women might feel proud and justified to be caring people since it can do a lot of good for the world if we have more care for each other. This suggests that when women are liberated and treated as equals, they will want to retain their virtue of care. However, there is also a recognition that distinctly 'feminine' virtues are socially constructed and that women have been assigned the caring role by a system of patriarchy that they seek to overturn. The unpaid labour of care is assigned to women, imposed upon them, and is thus another way in which sex as a binary is created and recreated. Feminism has helped us understand that care, far from being innate, has been co-opted into a tool of oppression.

Feminist science

When women are persistently praised for being carers, and men are praised for other 'virtues' (they are assertive, go-getters, breadwinners and so on), this becomes a self-fulfilling prophecy. As such, evolutionary biologists and psychologists are able to find evidence that confirms these beliefs about men and women, further reifying the idea of two distinct sexes. But feminist science has firmly debunked this line of enquiry, carefully unpicking and unpacking the biases and flawed underpinnings of what we thought was settled science about sex and sex differences.

For example, as Lucy Cooke explains in *Bitch* (2022):

Darwin's explanation for the constancy of his gendered sex roles is that it all boils down to fundamental differences between sperm and eggs. Sperm are mobile, he noted, while eggs are sedentary; and in this disparity lay the foundations for 'active' masculinity and 'passive' femininity.[2]

Darwin's work was later 'confirmed' by twentieth-century English geneticist Angus John Bateman, who Cooke explains wanted to 'offer an empirical lifeline' to Darwin's theories. In 1948 Bateman studied fruit flies, and from this extrapolated to humans, stating that the norm across the animal kingdom was for males to have 'an indiscriminating eagerness' and for females to demonstrate a 'discriminating passivity'.[3]

Cooke goes on to explain that 24 years later, despite Bateman's work having faded into obscurity, *evolutionary* biologist Robert Trivers cited Bateman as the key reference in what would be an extremely influential paper: 'Parental Investment and Sexual Selection'.[4] This quickly became the basis for a cascade of sex differences research, and renewed interest in old Victorian ideas about men and women. The idea that men are active and women are passive soon became a pervasive idea, seeping into science and popular culture once again. Cooke traces this spread from scientific articles through to *Playboy* magazine, which stated in 1979 that 'Recent scientific theory suggests there are innate differences between the sexes and what's right for the gander is wrong for the goose.' She also goes on to show how rape, infidelity and even intimate partner abuse became justified as 'adaptive traits' because of these theories.[5]

Bitch tells the story of how feminist scientist Patricia Gowaty dedicated her life's work to 'fearlessly questioning what she calls "the standard model" of sex differences in behaviour'.[6] Her work studying the eastern bluebird, *Sialia sialis*, provided proof that in this species the female was not simply passive, but rather played a very active role in owning their sexual destiny. Similarly, another feminist scientist, anthropologist Sarah Blaffer Hrdy, was 'the first person to challenge "the myth of the coy female" and is known by many as the original feminist Darwinist', according to Cooke.[7]

Hrdy went on to show that female primates are not simply passive, but rather extremely promiscuous and often have non-conceptive sex with multiple males. Her theory is that this is to manipulate male primates as a protection mechanism against infanticide that happens during troop takeovers. Cooke explains why this matters:

> Evolutionary biologists . . . may relish the idea that all women are ultimately seeking monogamy in order to provide the best support for their kids, but if women were so naturally inclined towards fidelity then why, wonders Hrdy, is their sexuality so culturally controlled? Whether the restraining tool is slanderous language, divorce or, worse, genital mutilation there is a near universal suspicion that women will engage in promiscuous sex if left unchecked. An alternative perspective, endorsed by Hrdy, sees the potency of female sexuality being such that patriarchal social systems evolved in order to curb and

confine it . . . One that cannot be divined by her fixed gametal destiny, however popular the paradigm, but is dependent on her circumstances, and the various options open to her.[8]

Because of this, it is helpful to reframe our thinking and to see the idea of 'feminine' and 'masculine' virtues (and 'male' and 'female' attributes) for what they are: a patriarchal mechanism to keep women separate, different and content with their subordinate position. To create the Other. It should come as no surprise that we feel that this is harmful: not only to women, but to men and gender expansive people too. Anyone has the capacity for care. Instead, we argue that the very idea of 'feminine' and 'masculine' virtues should be rejected. There are simply human virtues.

The choice we are left with, then, is: 1) the rejection of the version of womanhood imposed upon some people (womanhood as exclusively femininity/feminine virtues), including a rejection of care as a virtue; or 2) acceptance of care as a true virtue but, with it, apparent acceptance of the patriarchal construction of what it is to be a woman. Similarly for men and toxic masculinity.

Now let us consider how this plays out in the case of sport. One thing we might praise about *Women's Sport* is the lack of cheating and the generally honest spirit in which it is played. There is a seemingly better ethos than in *Sport*, which is afflicted with gamesmanship, where win-at-all-costs is embraced. *Women's Sport* may seem more attractive because the competitors show a compassion for each other and always put human decency first, above even victory. The dilemma raises itself here, though. Is this lack of ruthlessness, this meek acceptance of outcomes, win or lose, itself inculcated as a feminine virtue and a further indicator that women are not expected – perhaps not allowed – to take sport as seriously as men? In *Sport*, a supreme will to win above all else is considered admirable, indeed the very essence of *Sport* itself. But when those in *Women's Sport* take up this very same value, they are castigated for not setting a good example. Women, simply by virtue of being women, are not allowed to be ruthless. If we cast our thoughts back to Chapter Two, we will remember that women, particularly women in sport, must conform to a sanctioned version of sporting femininity. If she dares to transgress, for example by fully embodying the win-at-all-costs mindset, she will swiftly be met with the policing arm of patriarchy: misogyny. She will experience the full force of gender policing as a public warning to other women. Next time you hear deep public resentment about the actions of a sportswoman – such as when Serena Williams smashed her racket in competitive frustration, or regarding Caster Semenya being too good – notice the language used about her and ask yourself whether a sportsman doing the exact same thing would be met with the same reaction. *Women's Sport* seems expected to retain a naive charm that is long gone from the men's game.

From these expectations, and in this policing, a patriarchal seed is planted: the idea that *Women's Sport* – now positioned as the wholesome, family-friendly version of *Sport* – is different. This difference is then put on a pedestal and praised. We hear echoes of the complementarian view that difference is a virtue. Equal but different, they say. And so, *Women's Sport* is co-opted and moulded into a space where 'feminine' virtues should flourish. Must flourish. *Women's Sport* becomes a form of care work, taking on the labour of needing to reflect societal care as done by women. See how women footballers are expected to stay on the pitch and spend time meeting fans immediately after games, and the wrath they incur if they do what men do and go straight off to the showers.

It is important to notice how *Women's Sport* is thus further made into a tool that can promote patriarchal ideas about women, women's bodies and women's place and role in the world. Strong narratives about *Women's Sport* as being a space of liberation, of feminist wins and of women's empowerment fall flat in the face of this reality. Following Sara Ahmed, noticing becomes a feminist tool.[9]

We must, therefore, remain sceptical of alluring ideas of *Women's Sport* needing to maintain 'feminine' virtues. On the surface, once again, this narrative seems to be a feminist one: we care about care. But when we essentialize care and compassion and decency as exclusively feminine virtues, enacted in and by *Women's Sport*, and further expect only *Women's Sport* to uphold these, then we are reifying old, outdated patriarchal ideas about gender and gender difference. This is a very powerful form of gender policing and maintenance. Absolving men and *Sport* of their role in the labour of care does a disservice to men, too. It should be no surprise that so-called 'masculine' values of competition and ruthlessness become toxic in an environment where boys and men are excused from, or even condemned for, showing care towards others.

While it is a relatively straightforward argument to reject the notion of *Women's Sport* becoming more like *Sport*, it is a more complicated one to reject the opposite: men's *Sport* becoming more like *Women's Sport*. But just because it takes more steps does not mean that we should shy away from arguing the case. Feminist killjoys always take up that mantle. Care, compassion and decency are human virtues, open and available to all, we just don't teach them to boys or expect them of men. Similarly, competitiveness, drive and ambition, far from being 'masculine', are virtues also available to all.

Moving beyond this, we want to argue for a vision of *Feminist Sport*. But, first, we need to consider the argument for *Women's Sport* imagined not through the lens of feminine and masculine virtues, but as a space designed by women for women.

Women's Sport: By women for women

We are currently seeing the rise of women calling for *Women's Sport* to break away on its own. The prevailing idea here is that if *Women's Sport* can disentangle itself from the current structures of *Sport*, it will be able to set up and operate within new structures created by women for women. This will allow the creation of a contemporary vision for what *Women's Sport* can be. Such was the aim and purpose of the Women's Tennis Association (WTA), set up by Billie Jean King as one of the 'original 9' tennis players who split from the governing body to launch their own tour.

This sounds admirable. It even sounds like a plausible way forward. Indeed, it seems a feminist way forward. But just because people are women does not mean that they are feminists. The flaw here is in the retention of the binary.

When we preserve activities that are designed and designated for men and for women separately, we are upholding patriarchal ideas of 'real' men and 'real' women (as we discussed in Chapter Three), even if the justifications are on the grounds of equality of the sexes. This reinforces old, outdated ideas about the sex binary and sex differences. This can even occur if we make those spaces inclusive of gender expansive people, for the project is still underpinned by an idea that women, as a class, are different from men in key ways. Nurturing women and, or versus, toxic men is still the prevailing message. Protectionist arguments can still take hold, and sex-difference hype can be reinforced.

On this basis, we reject arguments for *Women's Sport* built by women, for women. Just because something is built by women does not mean that it is feminist. We are now ready to argue instead for a radical new vision of *Feminist Sport* that applies to all sport.

Feminist Sport: A radical proposal

We see *Feminist Sport* as an opportunity for the renegotiation of (sporting) values. Much as Descartes threw out all his beliefs, to start from scratch, just in case there were any bad ones that might infect the rest,[10] our response to the challenge of a radical vision for the future of sport is to cast out all the constraints and values that we associate with *Sport* and *Women's Sport* and decide what we want the sporting experience and our sporting values to be.

For us, *Feminist Sport* is not about women alone. It is about all of humanity. *Feminist Sport* rejects binary sex and the idea of sex difference as a basis for division. Rather, it is a radically inclusive space where all can flourish. On this, we are very much in agreement with Jennifer Doyle, although she still makes her point as a defence of *Women's Sport*. We have given our reasons for preferring *Feminist Sport*, and as such we substitute 'Feminist' for 'Women's' in the following, *mutatis mutandis*:

[*Feminist*] Sport is not a defensive structure from which men are excluded so that women might flourish. It is, in fact, the opposite of this: it is, potentially, a radically inclusive space which has the capacity to destroy the public's ideas about gender and gender difference precisely because gender is always in play in *Women's Sport* in ways that it is not in men's sports (with a few exceptions – e.g. figure skating). Because men have been so committed to the 'end of *Women's Sport*' for so long, [*Feminist Sport*] thrives in the zone of destruction. It has its own character thanks to the gender trouble at its origin. If [*Feminist*] *Sport* has one job that really is different from *Sport* and *Women's Sport*, it is the destruction of sex/gender difference. *Sport* and *Women's Sport* (with a few exceptions which prove the rule) reinforce ideologies of gender difference. [*Feminist*] *Sport* destroys them.[11]

Casting off the imposed categories of boys/men and girls/women, as well as notions of 'feminine' and 'masculine' virtues and values, *Feminist Sport* creates an opportunity for us to reimagine and recreate sport in radical new ways. What, then, are the feminist values from which we want to mould this new sport? And how might we then put structures in place that uphold those values?

Discarding unnecessary and unhelpful old chestnuts – such as the supposed conflict between safety, fairness and inclusion, or the idea that sport must be divided into boys/men and girls/women – can help us to have a new conversation from a different starting point. It is worth considering questions such as: who decided that safety, fairness and inclusion were the three core values of sport? What do each of these really stand for? Who is safety and fairness for, in this context? If we do decide to retain these values, how else might we approach them? How else might we divide sport up to ensure safety? What do we want to prioritize in and through sport? Asking new questions of old problems can help us to think through our underlying assumptions, and be generative in thinking about how we might advance sport as a feminist space in new ways.

While this might seem overly ambitious, the concept of *Feminist Sport* is not simply a naive thought experiment. While right now it may seem almost impossible to reimagine and recreate sport and sporting spaces with feminist, rather than patriarchal, ideals, we have seen this shift happen more broadly across society. A key example for us is the shift away from old, outdated ideas about sex differences. In most areas of education and work we no longer organize people around obsolete ideas, discussed before, of pink and blue brains (though of course this still bleeds through). Similarly, passé ideas about race and racial difference are largely rejected as a way of separating people (though it also has a very real presence and effect, and, like sexism and sex difference approaches, is strongly re-emerging).

Intersectional feminist scientists and activists have shown us new paths forward in these and many other domains. They have shown, for example, as Rachel E. Gross explains, that far from being about elevating (some) women at the expense of men, feminist approaches offer:

> a powerful set of tools for examining the history, context, and power structures in which scientific questions are asked. By bringing marginalized perspectives to the table, it can generate new questions and methodologies that help scientists identify and correct for hidden bias.

Think of it as a stake strapped to a growing tree: it provides scaffolding to help the tree get back on track when it starts to lean too far to one side.[12]

We see a feminist conception of sport as providing this stake: as a way of getting sport back on track to being a welcoming, safe, fulfilling space in which all can thrive.

Feminist Sport starts with feminist values and a feminist ethic of care: finding ways to create respectful spaces and experiences within and through sport. Feminism is also about establishing an ethos and practices by which everyone can be their full selves. For it is only when people feel safe to be and bring their full selves to the world that they can thrive. We envisage a world that goes beyond the boxes into which we put people: that liberates us from the cages of expectation placed on us because of how we present. *Feminist Sport* is a project that should foster belonging for all.

Feminist Sport means the destruction of those old norms, with an accompanying liberation not just for women but also for men and gender expansive people alike. Instead of narratives about sporting dominance, ruthlessness and humiliation we can emphasize values of care, nurturing, development, agency and liberty. Many are turned off by sport because it feels like one has to wear a straightjacket to participate. *Feminist Sport* shows us that it needn't be that way. This is a feature that should be retained in the future of sport.

Erasing women?

Any discussion of decentring sex/gender in the ways in which we organize society inevitably surfaces very real but, as we'll show, ultimately unfounded fears of the erasure of women. All too often, when we propose the idea of moving away from the categories of *Sport* and *Women's Sport* and towards an idea of desegregated gender-inclusive sport we are met with worries about the progress that women in sport have made. These valid anxieties include the loss of opportunities for girls and women, reservations about girls and women losing dedicated spaces for their physical development, and trepidations about unravelling the critical mass that women have attained in participation in sport and in the boardroom.

This is where a feminist killjoy noticing is, once again, instructive. Rather than thinking about these as potential losses or costs, could we rehabilitate our understanding of them through a feminist lens? We think we can.

Drawing on the grand arguments that we have made throughout this book, we can now join together the dots to reveal the overall pattern. *Sport* has always been a patriarchal tool for the division of people into two sexes, and *Women's Sport* was more recently instituted as a further mechanism for segregation. This segregation has created the site of strict gender policing. *Women's Sport*, far from being a feminist win, is a patriarchal apparatus.

We could attempt to co-opt *Women's Sport* for feminist goals, including fighting to create more opportunities for women. But because of the loaded history of the category, it will always be more challenging to truly make *Women's Sport* into a feminist ideal – even if its structures are separated from men's *Sport* and run by women for women.

Fears about erasing women play into this very narrative by once again essentializing women and painting them as needing protection from men. It also strongly upholds the sex-essentialist gender binary. Because of this, we believe there is an urgent need to reject the current structures, and to put fear-mongering about erasing women into context as part of patriarchal control. So if we do reject boys/men and girls/women as our primary categories for sporting participation and activity, how do we ensure that our feminist values are upheld? Here we follow academic Dean Spade:

> I certainly believe that we can move toward de-regulating gender and still engage in important corrective practices like gender-based affirmative action. I am not arguing for a gender-blind society in which all people are similarly androgynous, but instead for a world in which diverse gender expressions and identities occur, but none are punished and membership in these categories is used less and less to distribute rights and privileges.[13]

Feminist Sport thus, by decentring and deregulating gender as the primary structure within which sport is administered, allows us to ensure that everyone has an equitable opportunity for participation and, ultimately, thriving. Using an equity lens helps us to not ignore those groups that have suffered historical injustices. Women and other marginalized groups of people have been assigned a subordinate position in patriarchal power structures and we think *Feminist Sport* has a case for restorative justice while those structures are being dismantled.

Values of *Feminist Sport*

Next, we want to consider some examples of values in sport, the way in which they are and have been made gender-specific, and how we could proceed to rethink them as values we may want to see in *Feminist Sport*.

Cath Bishop, writing in 2023 in *The Guardian* newspaper, identified a value that we feel ought to be a part of *Feminist Sport*. This value is compassion. Bishop is herself a triple Olympian and now a leadership and culture coach. She recommends a culture of compassion not just because it is a good human value in itself, but also because it gets us better outcomes in sport.[14] And, of course, everyone would benefit from a culture of compassion.

Bishop points out the roots of (men's) *Sport* in the Victorian public school system and how it could be used as a preparation for the military, for leadership roles and for other dominant patriarchal vocations. The stiff-upper-lip response to sporting adversity can then be applied generally, outside of sporting contexts. There should be no complaints in defeat, even when it is undeserved, and no mercy shown to the weak. In *Sport*, one is always allowed to take advantage of an opponent's weakness. If your badminton rival slips, you are perfectly entitled, indeed expected, to smash a shot where they will have no chance of reaching it. It is alarming to think of a nascent Victorian *Sport* inculcating such values in the next generation of leaders, although it does explain much of what has followed since. *Sport* rewarded mercilessness. It fostered tough ruthlessness as the essential attribute of success.

But is it really like this? Coaches now see instead that a compassionate approach can gain better results since players who are safe to recognize their weaknesses and vulnerabilities are far more likely to gain the directed support that they need to improve their performance. In simple terms, where sport is founded on a fear of failure, athletes do not flourish since this is an entirely negative approach to sport, where the athlete must develop a defensive strategy so as to avoid at all costs the humiliation of defeat. Better results seem possible where, instead, one develops a positive compassionate approach, without fear of failure, where the athletes enjoy the play and can see it as an important part of their personal growth, involving self-love and care but also love and care for others.

This is an important lesson. Sport is a social activity. In a profound way, it is a collaboration, even where it sets us in opposition to each other. One cannot really play tennis, or football, or even have a foot race, alone. Sport involves an othering of one's opponents, but there also has to be a respect for their agency and consent in allowing us to join them in a collective activity: to do things with them that neither of us can do alone. Team sports, races and any major competition will involve multiple players, allowing us to participate with them in a way that helps us and in which we help them. By adding the competitive edge, pride in front of others and prospect of social approval, we improve ourselves as athletes. We attain better times, distances and heights. We develop new skills that we would not acquire without the social nature of sport. We should have no contempt for our opponents. We should love them for allowing us to realize our own sporting ambitions.

Compassion is a feminist act. Chloe Kelly (again!) attracted attention after scoring the winning shoot-out penalty against Nigeria at the 2023 World Cup. Instead of running to celebrate and take the personal glory, she quietly went to console the distraught opposing goalkeeper, Chiamaka Nnadozie. Kelly was a winner, but she recognized that Nnadozie's efforts to stop her were a precondition of her own victory.

Sport is so often founded on a central idea of competition that we lose sight of the extent to which it is fundamentally a collaboration. Not just teammates', but everyone's cooperation is essential to the contest. We must recognize the humanity of others, their struggle, and not dehumanize the loser as faceless and a mere means to an end. Where avoidance of failure is no longer the motivation, so too can we compassionately forgive mistakes, and indeed own up to them. As we move towards a *Feminist Sport*, this is a value we should seek to foster.

Sport is not only about playing. Most of our engagements with sport will be through watching, and here we have seen feminist values emerge too. It is, after all, a form of entertainment, an interest, a hobby, and occasionally all-consuming for the fans. This shows why *Feminist Sport* matters. Consuming the segregated versions of *Sport* and *Women's Sport* plays a significant role in shaping our views of what both men and women are and can be. A wider representation, where we see athletes play sport regardless of their gender, has the ability to destroy our ideas about sex differences, and thus build a world in which physicality is for everyone. If you can see it, you can be it.

Writing for The Conversation website about the development of fans' groups for the Matildas – the Australian women's football team – Kasey Symons and Paul Bowell note how the team attracted fans who would previously have felt alienated by the fan culture of *Sport*.[15] Certain ways of supporting a team have developed in *Sport* that can be regarded as excluding and toxic. There are specific modes of behaving in stadiums that are socially enforced to ensure conformity. For instance, in men's football, one is not allowed to support, or even admit liking, any other team. One has to behave in an unwelcoming or aggressive way to opposition players and fans, which has sometimes spilled over into violence. In contrast, *Feminist Sport* would allow fans to follow what we saw at the 2023 Football World Cup; that is: 'Fans also felt they could do things such as change teams and support multiple teams. People were fans of the competition more broadly and also wanted to generally support women playing the sport they love.'[16]

Symons and Bowell emphasize the inclusivity of *Women's Sport*. It has developed a fan culture in which there would be few concerns about taking young children to the big games, where LGBTQ+ fans feel that they can be themselves without fear, and where women would feel comfortable attending alone. This is confirmed in our own experiences at women's games. Many fans wear rainbow scarves, showing that they are either allies of, or part of, queer communities. They do so with unquestioned acceptance, in comfort, indeed pride, knowing that it is a safe space with negligible personal danger. Trans supporters use their bathroom of choice without alarm or incident. Fans of different teams mingle without hostility. *Women's Sport* is a welcoming space where all can be included, since in supporting *Women's Sport* they are signalling their own acceptance of diversity as a value. We feel in good conscience that we can recommend watching *Women's Sport* to anyone who has previously felt excluded or intimidated at the thought of mixing with other fans. Even in football, with its history of violence, there is now a very different feel at the women's games. And why should people feel excluded from sport? It can, after all, be spectacular, engrossing, uplifting, and even just the sense of community, being surrounded by thousands of other like-minded people, is important for us as social beings. Why should that sense of community be the preserve of masculinity? Indeed, queer folk, who have been excluded from so much historically, perhaps need to be part of such a community even more. Events in which queerness is normal, and inclusion comes regardless of who you are, have been rare enough in wider society but even more so in sport. Now we see that changing.

It might be wondered why this fan culture has formed around *Women's Sport* in particular. Is it just a pure accident, perhaps where excluded sports enthusiasts have gathered together by chance? Or is there something in the nature of *Women's Sport* that explains why it has attracted an inclusive fan base? We will make the case for the latter and can state our reasons in either a superficial or a more considered way.

Here is the superficial explanation. There is more open queerness among women playing sport than there is among men playing sport, which immediately signals it as an inclusive space to potential fans. A number of women who play sport have let it be known that they are not heterosexual, for instance, and are now willing to show themselves to be gender non-conforming (though never *too* non-conforming, as we have discussed). This makes it much easier for fans to emulate the athletes that they watch and support. For how could fans face discrimination for being queer when everyone is there to support and extol players many of whom are themselves queer? In contrast, men's *Sport* has a history of compulsory heterosexuality. Stephen has personal experience of this, witnessing plenty of homophobic 'jokes' and 'banter' in the locker room. 'Queer' was used as a term of abuse, along with a host of other derogatory terms. Men's *Sport* has been a breeding ground for toxic masculinity, with strict gender conformity enforced mercilessly. In the few cases where sportsmen did come out as gay, they paid a heavy price, as in the devastating example of Justin Fashanu. This made it harder still for future gay athletes to be themselves, especially in sports that were considered tough and macho. Because of the gender trouble at its origin, *Women's Sport* is not afflicted as much with this problem. The fandom reflects this diversity among the competitors. Again, if you can see it, you can be it.

The deeper explanation of the diversity of fans of *Women's Sport* makes the same point but with a more politicized angle. This is that the very nature of *Women's Sport* is subversive, requiring a transgression of the binary gender norms, and its mere existence is an act of defiance against patriarchy.

Given what we have outlined previously in this book, it should be clear why we speak in these terms. Women have had to fight to be included in sport, including challenging the very idea of what it means to be a woman. Women were supposed to be delicate, non-physical and primarily destined for child-rearing, hence not naturally suitable for sports. Often one's peak sporting years coincide with one's expected reproductive years, so electing to play sport became an affront to that latter role. Those who pay heed to women in sport cannot fail to see strong, confident women who have refused to accept the norms of delicacy and frailty that they were prescribed. This is why women in sport can so easily be an inspiration, particularly to queer folk, who see someone to emulate: someone who has not been constrained by what society would have allotted them but has rejected the dominant gender norms so as to be who they want to be. To that extent, it is of the nature of *Women's Sport* to be queer, so no wonder that it attracts queer fans: people who assert their freedom to make of their lives what they want, unconstrained by the dominant gendered expectations.

These are some of the positive values that have emerged from *Women's Sport*, and they emerge because women playing sport is an immediate act of transgression. Nevertheless, for all the reasons we have been outlining, the category of *Women's Sport* remains problematic and not something that we wish to sustain. We must recognize how the policing arm of patriarchy kicks in to monitor and regulate any person in *Women's Sport* who is *too* gender non-conforming, for example. *Women's Sport*, due to its origin, is still a mechanism for patriarchal control. This is why we advocate for *Feminist Sport* unencumbered of the constabulary of *Women's Sport* that is sex-segregation.

The renegotiation of values

We have given a flavour of the opportunity for a renegotiation of values brought by the argument for *Feminist Sport* that we put forward. The feminist killjoy has always questioned the status quo. Part of the challenge to the status quo is to the dominant values of sport: values that are then spread further afield, outside of sporting contexts. We have argued, then, for the desegregation of sport along gender lines, and for a new vision of gender-inclusive *Feminist Sport*. What we want is a *Feminist Sport* that is free of sex-specific values. What is right and wrong for one should be right or wrong for all.

To resolve our original dilemma from earlier in this chapter: it is not simply a case of advocating for traditional feminine virtues and seeking to retain them once women attain liberation from the patriarchal category of *Women's Sport*. On the contrary, our vision of *Feminist Sport* requires that norms of traditional femininity and masculinity are overturned, not least the norm that women are not meant to be physically robust but, instead, delicate and demure.

The values which we carry into *Feminist Sport* will thus be values of social justice: of inclusion and acceptance; of liberation for all, including men and queer people; of equity and equality, including equality of wealth and of power and of race; and of compassion for others, especially the 'others', recognizing sport as a collaborative activity that can raise and nourish us all.

The fight for equality in sport is a social justice fight, where mere participation is itself a political act, and women and queer people in sport have always been political. Upon her retirement from international soccer, Megan Rapinoe, interviewed for *The Atlantic* in 2023, acknowledged this, saying: 'What I've realized for a long time is that we're playing two games at the same time. One, we're playing all against each other. And then the other one, we're all playing together to win equality and progress and what we deserve.'[17] This is consistent with so much that we have written above, in this chapter and before. There is a reason women and queer athletes support each other so strongly, why they show compassion even to their opponents, and why fans have no shame in supporting more than one team or switching allegiances. They acknowledge that it is a shared struggle where success for one is a success for all. While defeat is never the aim, where one is beaten by opponents who themselves show just what women can achieve, and how far they can go, it benefits all women. In such a context, what we all need are not smaller goals but bigger and bigger ones.

Returning to our old friend, Mr Mason, we see how far we have progressed since the gentleman declared that 'Woman was not made to be the rival of man in any sphere or position of life.

Men and women should not stand in unwholesome competition.'[18] It is no surprise, with such attitudes, that the Victorians originally sought to exclude women from sport. In due course, *Women's Sport* emerged as the compromise position. But it was only what patriarchy was willing to allow. Let us now, instead, insist that this was no more than an intermediate stage on the path to true equality: true equality that only *Feminist Sport* would give us.

We have outlined the values on which *Feminist Sport* should be founded. Is this too radical, perhaps? Would the authorities of *Sport* ever allow such a seismic shift in their organization of sport, to allow a new, gender-neutral sport? In that case, are our proposals entirely too ambitious and, therefore, unrealistic? Such a judgement is, in fact, exactly what we would expect. The first response of power, whenever it is challenged, will be to mock and belittle, to discourage opposition and instil apathy. This stops most challenges in their tracks, preventing them from gaining any traction.

Feminist Sport will not go away, however. Indeed, a feminist future is the only future for which it is worth preparing. In that case, we are confident that if we have any future readers, they will be looking back on this book from a feminist world in which patriarchy has been overthrown. Their sport will be *Feminist Sport*. Men and women will be equals in both mental and physical respects, although once they are, gender categories might have disappeared altogether. Human flourishing and, for that matter, human rights will truly be for all. The alternative is that neither we, nor any other writers, have any future readers at all.

We have identified *Women's Sport* as a patriarchal creation, as a cage in which to imprison women, as a segregated space with no voluntary exit. Dividing people into two groups, this creation sets up conditions for unequal treatment: for vastly different levels of resourcing, which then unsurprisingly produces differential outcomes between those two groups. This is what we oppose. Presenting women with smaller goals is never going to see them attaining the same levels that men can achieve. Then, as we noted, the unequal outcomes generated by the system – the sexual division of sport – will be used to justify the same system of unequal treatment.

This argument, simple yet challenging as it is, has been presented in successive chapters, from retrospective, historical, scientific, inclusion, justice and prospective angles. Novel ideas bear repeating so we have approached our topic from all directions. We asked of our readers an open mind and a commitment to equality. We are grateful to those who proceeded and continued in that spirit.

Are there signs of hope that the changes for which we advocate might indeed occur? We think so. The RFEF (the Spanish Football Federation) could not have handled the fallout from their World Cup win any worse. But one change that the players negotiated was positive. It was agreed that the term 'women's football' would be dropped. Both the men's and women's teams would now be called simply the 'Spanish football team'. The language was degendered even if the teams themselves were not yet. Such a move is significant. Was this a genuine acceptance of the issues around inequality by the RFEF? Time will tell the extent of this particular victory. We look forward to more and more like it, however, since the era of *Feminist Sport* has only just begun.

References

Preface

1 Christine Delphy, *Close to Home: A Materialist Analysis of Women's Oppression* (London, 2016).
2 bell hooks, *Feminism Is for Everybody* (New York, 2015).

1 The Sports Bra

1 For the quotations from Coubertin, we are indebted to Stephen's student Mary Atkinson, who in some cases translated from the original French, since Coubertin's most sexist and racist works have not yet appeared in English. A valuable source is Dikaia Chatziefstathiou, 'Reading Baron Pierre de Coubertin: Issues of Gender and Race', *Aethlon: The Journal of Sport Literature*, xxv/2 (2008), pp. 95–116. In English, there is Coubertin's *Olympism: Selected Writings*, ed. N. Müller, International Olympic Committee (Lausanne, 2000). See also V. Girginov and S. J. Parry, *The Olympic Games Explained: A Student Guide to the Evolution of the Modern Olympic Games* (London, 2005). The 'unsuitable for females' quotation is from the English FA itself, 'The Story of Women's Football in England', www.thefa.com, accessed 9 May 2024.
2 Shireen Ahmed, quoted in Julia Belas Tindade, '"It's brutal" – How French Football's Hijab Ban Is Affecting Muslim Women', *The Guardian*, www.theguardian.com, 4 May 2022.
3 Brandi Chastain with Gloria Averbuch, *It's Not About the Bra* (New York, 2004).
4 bell hooks, *Feminism Is for Everybody* (New York, 2015), p. 31.
5 On the invention of the sports bra, from one of the inventors, see Lisa Lindahl, *Unleash the Girls* (Charleston, SC, 2019).
6 Deborah Linton, 'Lioness Chloe Kelly's Sports Bra Celebration was a Lesson in Liberation', *British Vogue*, www.vogue.co.uk, 1 August 2022.

7 For more on the Sports Bra bar in Portland, see Zoha Fatima, 'The "Sports Bra" Bar That Shows Only Women's Sports Is Inspiring Girls in the Community', https://scoop.upworthy.com, 11 May 2023.

8 This Alex Scott quotation is the authors' own transcription, from the broadcast of the BBC's post-match coverage.

9 Sedona Prince's viral video showing the (comically) different weight training facilities for men and women can be found on TikTok, where she is @sedonerrr.

10 Simone de Beauvoir, *The Second Sex* [1949], trans. Constance Borde and Sheila Malovany-Chevallier (London, 2011), p. 293.

11 Angela Saini, *The Patriarchs* (London, 2023), pp. 6–7.

2 Sport Is a Feminist Issue

1 Sara Ahmed, *The Feminist Killjoy Handbook* (London, 2023), pp. 1–2.

2 See the inside jacket of Ahmed's *The Feminist Killjoy Handbook*.

3 Ellyn Kestnbaum, *Culture on Ice: Figure Skating and Cultural Meaning* (Middletown, CT, 2003), pp. 68–9.

4 Beverley Smith, *Figure Skating: A Celebration* (Toronto, 1994), pp. 20–21.

5 For the strict gender binary as a fascist project, we have drawn on Kate Manne, *Down Girl: The Logic of Misogyny* (London, 2019), and Jason Stanley, *How Fascism Works: The Politics of Us and Them* (New York, 2018).

6 Quote from the National Baseball Hall of Fame, 'The History of Women in Baseball', https://baseballhall.org, accessed 9 May 2024.

7 Babe Ruth quoted in Brian Cronin, 'Sports Legend Revealed: Did a Female Pitcher Strike Out Babe Ruth and Lou Gehrig?', archived blog post available at www.latimes.com, 23 February 2011.

8 Ibid.

9 On the story of Jackie Mitchell Gilbert, see Michael Aubrecht, 'Jackie Mitchell – The Pride of the Yankees', www.baseball-almanac.com, November 2003, and Cronin, 'Sports Legend Revealed'. On the disbanding of the Vasser baseball team, see the National Baseball Hall of Fame website, 'The History of Women in Baseball'. This includes the quotation about parents' concerns for the safety of their daughters.

10 Zhang quoted on the Olympics website, 'Zhang Shan: The Only Female Shooter to Win Gold in a Mixed Competition', www.olympics.com, 5 July 2020.

11 See Jonathan Selvaraj, '10m Air Rifle: The Olympic Sport Where Women Outgun Men', www.espn.com, 18 July 2021.

12 See Bobbi Gibb, 'A Run of One's Own', www.runningpast.com, accessed 31 January 2024.

13 Tom Sewell, 'Roberta: "I Ran Race for Fun"', *Boston Traveler*, 20 April 1966.

13 Ahmed, *The Feminist Killjoy Handbook*, p. 269.

14 See Gibb, 'A Run of One's Own'.

15 There is now a rich literature on British football for women but we would like to draw attention to Stefan Mårtensson, 'Branding Women's Football in a Field of Hegemonic Masculinity', *Entertainment and Sports Law Journal*, VIII/5 (2010), pp. 1–45.

16 See The FA 'Kicking Down Barriers: The Story of Women's Football in England', www.thefa.com, accessed 29 February 2024.

17 Shelley Alexander, 'Trail-Blazers Who Pioneered Women's Football', *BBC News*, http://news.bbc.co.uk, 3 June 2005.

18 On whether women's football should have smaller pitches, balls and goals, there are many reports and discussions on the Internet. One of t he better articles is from the BBC, highlighting then Chelsea manager Emma Hayes's support for the idea: 'The Players Podcast: England's Fara Williams and Lucy Bronze on Comparisons to Men's Games', www.bbc.co.uk, 17 March 2021. This puts her in the same company as the (notorious) former (men's) footballer Joey Barton, unfortunately.

19 Heinz Reinkemeier, quoted in Selvaraj, '10m Air Rifle'.

20 'Paula Radcliffe Wins Battle to Keep Marathon World Record', *Daily Mirror*, www.mirror.co.uk, 11 November 2011.

21 Maggie Mertens, 'This Woman Surfed the Biggest Wave of the Year', *The Atlantic*, www.theatlantic.com, 12 September 2020.

22 Ibid.

23 Ibid.

3 Policing Women's Sport

1 On the question 'What is a woman?', and experts' concerns about female eligibility policies, see Anna Posbergh, 'Defining "Woman": A Governmentality Analysis of How Protective Policies Are Created in Elite Women's Sport', *International Review for the Sociology of Sport*, LVII/8 (2022), pp. 1350–70.

2 Ernest Mason, *Womanhood in the God-Man* (London, 1891), pp. 9–12.

3 Ibid., pp. 18–19.

4 Bernard Suits, *The Grasshopper: Games, Life and Utopia*, 2nd edn (Peterborough, ON, 2005).

5 Mason, *Womanhood in the God-Man*, p. 28.

6 Ibid., p. 26.

7 See Lucy Cooke, *Bitch* (London, 2022) for Darwin's view on women.

8 Mason, *Womanhood in the God-Man*, pp. 33–4.

9 Mireia Garcés de Marcilla Musté, 'You Ain't Woman Enough: Tracing the Policing of Intersexuality in Sports and the Clinic', *Social and Legal Studies*, XXXI/6 (2022), pp. 847–70 (p. 848).

10 Eduardo Hay, 'Sex Determination in Putative Female Athletes', *Journal of the American Medical Association*, CCXXXI/9 (1972), pp. 998–9.

11 J. L. Simpson et al., 'Gender Verification in the Olympics', *JAMA*, CCLXXXIV/12 (2000), pp. 1568–9.

12 M. Genel and A. Ljungqvist, 'Essay: Gender Verification of Female Athletes', *The Lancet*, CCCLXIV, Special Issue (2005), S41.

13 Reuters, 'Semenya Offered to Show Her Body to Officials to Prove She Was Female', www.reuters.com, 24 May 2022.

14 Ruth Pearce, Sonja Erikainen and Ben Vincent, 'TERF Wars: An Introduction', *Sociological Review*, LXVIII/4 (2020), pp. 677–98.

15 Karkazis quotation from Lito Howse, 'Dr. Katrina Karkazis Discusses Rethinking the Popular Understanding of Testosterone', *Xtra*, www.xtra-magazine.com, 7 January 2022.

16 On sex testing, see Cara Tannenbaum and Sheree Bekker, 'Sex, Gender, and Sports', *BMJ*, CCCLXIV (2019), i1120.

17 Posbergh, 'Defining "Woman"'.

18 P. Fénichel et al., 'Molecular Diagnosis of 5α-Reductase Deficiency in 4 Elite Young Female Athletes through Hormonal Screening for Hyperandrogenism', *Journal of Clinical Endocrinology and Metabolism*, XCVIII/6 (2013), pp. 1055–9.

19 See Human Rights Watch Report, 'They're Chasing Us Away from Sport', www.hrw.org, 4 December 2020.

20 Rebecca Jordan Young and Katrina Karkazis, *Testosterone: An Unauthorized Biography* (Cambridge, MA, 2019), p. 169.

21 Tannenbaum and Bekker, 'Sex, Gender, and Sports'.

22 Celia Roberts, 'Tanner's Puberty Scale: Exploring the Historical Entanglements of Children, Scientific Photography and Sex', *Sexualities*, XIX/3 (2016), pp. 328–46 (p. 339). This draws on her 'Early Puberty and Public Health: A Social Scientific Pinboard', *Critical Public Health*, XX/4 (2010), pp. 429–38.

23 Roberts, 'Tanner's Puberty Scale', p. 339.

24 Sharda Ugra, 'World Athletics, Please Note: DSD Regulations are a Violation of Human Rights', *Hindustan Times*, www.hindustantimes.com, 5 December 2020.

25 See Frankie de la Cretaz, 'Attacks on Transgender Athletes Are Threatening Women's Sports', *Glamour*, www.glamour.com, 22 March 2021.

26 Katrina Karkazis and Morgan Carpenter, 'Impossible "Choices": The Inherent Harms of Regulating Women's Testosterone in Sport', *Bioethical Inquiry*, XV/4 (2018), pp. 579–87.

27 Margo Mountjoy et al., 'International Olympic Committee Consensus Statement: Harassment and Abuse (Non-Accidental Violence) in Sport', *British Journal of Sports Medicine*, L/17 (2016), pp. 1019–29.

4 Being in Your Body

1 For a study of those who are socially excluded from sport, see R. Spaaij, K. Farquharson and T. Marjoribanks, 'Sport and Social Inequalities', *Sociology Compass*, IX/5 (2015), pp. 400–411.

2 On the nature of sport, and what makes something a sport, Bernard Suits, *The Grasshopper: Games, Life and Utopia*, 2nd edn (Peterborough, ON, 2005) is a classic source, in which a game is defined and the place of games in a good human life outlined.

3 See, on the capabilities approach to human flourishing, Martha Nussbaum, *Creating Capabilities* (Cambridge, MA, 2011), which is the best source on the subject. Nussbaum acknowledges the importance of economist Amartya Sen as the origin of this view.

4 Frederick Hollick, *The Diseases of Woman: Their Causes and Cure Familiarly Explained* (New York, 1847), p. 199.

5 Ibid., p. 205.

6 See Kathleen McCrone, *Playing the Game: Sport and the Physical Emancipation of English Women, 1870–1914* (Lexington, KY, 1988). McCrone makes use of Donald Walker's 1836 *Exercises for Ladies*, republished by Penguin, 2018: a period piece.

7 IOC Medical Commission, Working Group, Women in Sport, 'Position Statement on Girls and Women in Sport, www.stillmed.olympic.org, 20 April 2002.

8 For more on roller derby, see Adele Pavlidis and Simone Fullagar, *Sport, Gender and Power: The Rise of Roller Derby* (Farnham and Burlington, VT, 2014). But for an informal introductory taster, Pet Shop Boys' official video for their song 'Winner' is freely available on YouTube.

9 Angela Saini, *Inferior: The True Power of Women and the Science that Shows It* (London, 2017).

10 This quotation, together with an account of the events, is from 'Spanish Football Federation Accused of Faking Jenni Hermoso's Statement on "Unacceptable" Kiss', www.euronews.com, 23 August 2023.

11 Tweet from Leah Williamson (@leahcwilliamson), 25 August 2023 on Twitter (now X).

12 Kate Manne, *Down Girl: The Logic of Misogyny* (London, 2019).

5 Beyond the Binary

1 Mary Wollstonecraft, *A Vindication of the Rights of Woman* [1792] (Oxford, 2008), p. 202.

2 For more on a 'human rights-based approach', see the UN Sustainable Development Group's statement at https://unsdg.un.org, accessed 31 January 2024.

3 Ibid.

4 Cinzia Rizzi and Michael Daventry, 'Star Skier Lindsey Vonn's Frustration at Not Being Allowed to Compete Against Men', www.euronews.com, 25 October 2019.

5 Audre Lorde, *The Master's Tools Will Never Dismantle the Master's House* (London, 2018).

6 Angela Saini, *The Patriarchs* (London, 2023).

7 Jean-Jacques Rousseau, 'Discourse on the Origin of Inequality', in *The Social Contract and Discourses*, trans. G.D.H. Cole (London, 1973), p. 99.

8 Wollstonecraft, *A Vindication of the Rights of Woman*, p. 155.

6 The Future of Feminist Sport

1 Mary Wollstonecraft, *A Vindication of the Rights of Woman* [1792] (Oxford, 2008).

2 Lucy Cooke, *Bitch* (London, 2022), p. 47.

3 Ibid., p. 50.

4 Robert Trivers, 'Parental Investment and Sexual Selection', in *Sexual Selection and the Descent of Man, 1871–1971*, ed. B. Campbell (Chicago, IL, 1972), pp. 136–79.

5 Cooke, *Bitch*, p. 51.

6 Ibid., p. 55.

7 Ibid., p. 59.

8 Ibid., p. 67.

9 Sara Ahmed, *The Feminist Killjoy Handbook* (London, 2023).

10 René Descartes, *Meditations on First Philosophy* [1641] (Cambridge, 2017).

11 The Jennifer Doyle quotation, which we adapt, is to be found in her essay 'Capturing Semenya', at https://thesportspectacle.com, 16 August 2016.

12 Rachel E. Gross, 'Feminist Science Is Not an Oxymoron', https://undark.org, 15 September 2022. We also recommend her book *Vagina Obscura: An Anatomical Voyage* (New York, 2022).

13 Dean Spade, 'Resisting Medicine, Re/modeling Gender', *Berkeley Women's Law Journal*, XVIII/1 (2003), pp. 15–37 (p. 29). We also recommend Ben Vincent's informative *Non-Binary Genders: Navigating Communities, Identities and Healthcare* (Bristol, 2020), and Dean's work

published in the *Transgender Studies Reader*, ed. Susan Stryker and Stephen Whittle (London, 2013).

14 Cath Bishop, 'Compassion can Produce Better Performance – Just Look at the Lionesses', *The Guardian*, www.theguardian.com, 14 August 2023.

15 Kasey Symons and Paul Bowell, '"Felt Alienated by the Men's Game": How the Culture of Women's Sport has Driven Record Matildas Viewership', www.theconversation.com, 16 August 2023.

16 Ibid.

17 Franklin Foer, 'Megan Rapinoe Answers the Critics', *The Atlantic*, www.theatlantic.com, 22 August 2023.

18 Ernest Mason, *Womanhood in the God-Man* (London, 1891), p. 34.

Bibliography

1 The Sports Bra

Chatziefstathiou, Dikaia, 'Reading Baron Pierre de Coubertin: Issues of Gender and Race', *Aethlon: The Journal of Sport Literature*, XXV/2 (2008), pp. 95–116

Coubertin, Pierre de, *Olympism: Selected Writings*, ed. N. Müller, International Olympic Committee (Lausanne, 2000)

Fatima, Zoha, 'The "Sports Bra" Bar That Shows Only Women's Sports Is Inspiring Girls in the Community', https://scoop.upworthy.com, 11 May 2023

Girginov, V., and S. J. Parry, *The Olympic Games Explained: A Student Guide to the Evolution of the Modern Olympic Games* (London, 2005)

Lindahl, Lisa, *Unleash the Girls* (Charleston, SC, 2019)

Manne, Kate, *Unshrinking* (London, 2024)

Young, Iris Marion, 'Throwing Like a Girl: A Phenomenology of Feminine Body Comportment Motility and Spatiality', *Human Studies*, III/1 (1980), pp. 137–56

2 Sport Is a Feminist Issue

Ahmed, Sara, *The Feminist Killjoy Handbook* (London, 2023)

Alexander, Shelley, 'Trail-Blazers Who Pioneered Women's Football', *BBC News*, http://news.bbc.co.uk, 3 June 2005

Aubrecht, Michael, 'Jackie Mitchell – The Pride of the Yankees', www.baseball-almanac.com, November 2003

Cronin, Brian, 'Sports Legend Revealed: Did a Female Pitcher Strike Out Babe Ruth and Lou Gehrig?', archived blog post available at www.latimes.com, 23 February 2011

Gibb, Bobbi, 'A Run of One's Own', www.runningpast.com, accessed 31 January 2024

Kestnbaum, Ellyn, *Culture on Ice: Figure Skating and Cultural Meaning* (Middletown, CT, 2003)

Manne, Kate, *Down Girl: The Logic of Misogyny* (London, 2019)

Mårtensson, Stefan, 'Branding Women's Football in a Field of Hegemonic Masculinity', *Entertainment and Sports Law Journal*, VIII/5 (2010), pp. 1–45

Mertens, Maggie, 'This Woman Surfed the Biggest Wave of the Year', *The Atlantic*, www.theatlantic.com, 12 September 2020

National Baseball Hall of Fame, 'The History of Women in Baseball', https://baseballhall.org, accessed 9 May 2024

Ryan, Joan, *Little Girls in Pretty Boxes: The Making and Breaking of Elite Gymnasts and Figure Skaters* [1995], 2nd edn (London, 2000)

Selvaraj, Jonathan, '10m Air Rifle: The Olympic Sport Where Women Outgun Men', www.espn.com, 18 July 2021

Sewell, Tom, 'Roberta: "I Ran Race for Fun"', *Boston Traveler*, 20 April 1966

Smith, Beverley, *Figure Skating: A Celebration* (Toronto, 1994)

Stanley, Jason, *How Fascism Works: The Politics of Us and Them* (New York, 2018)

3 Policing Women's Sport

Cooke, Lucy, *Bitch* (London, 2022)

Cretaz, Frankie de la, 'Attacks on Transgender Athletes Are Threatening Women's Sports', *Glamour*, www.glamour.com, 22 March 2021

Fénichel, P., et al., 'Molecular Diagnosis of 5α-Reductase Deficiency in 4 Elite Young Female Athletes through Hormonal Screening for Hyperandrogenism', *Journal of Clinical Endocrinology and Metabolism*, XCVIII/6 (2013), pp. 1055–9

Garcés de Marcilla Musté, Mireia, 'You Ain't Woman Enough: Tracing the Policing of Intersexuality in Sports and the Clinic', *Social and Legal Studies*, XXXI/6 (2022), pp. 847–70

Genel, M., and A. Ljungqvist, 'Essay: Gender Verification of Female Athletes', *The Lancet*, CCCLXVI, Special Issue (2005), S41

Ha, N. Q., et al., 'Hurdling over Sex? Sport, Science, and Equity', *Archives of Sexual Behavior*, XLIII/6 (2014), pp. 1035–42

Howse, Lito, 'Dr. Katrina Karkazis Discusses Rethinking the Popular Understanding of Testosterone', *Xtra*, www.xtramagazine.com, 7 January 2022

Human Rights Watch Report, 'They're Chasing Us Away from Sport', www.hrw.org, 4 December 2020

Jordan-Young, Rebecca, and Karkazis, Katrina, *Testosterone: An Unauthorized Biography* (Cambridge, MA, 2019)

Karkazis, Katrina, and M. Carpenter, 'Impossible "Choices": The Inherent
  Harms of Regulating Women's Testosterone in Sport', *Bioethical Inquiry*,
  VI (2018), pp. 579–87

Mason, Ernest, *Womanhood in the God-Man* (London, 1891)

Pearce, Ruth, S. Erikainen and B. Vincent, 'TERF Wars: An Introduction',
  Sociological Review, LXVIII/4 (2020), pp. 677–98

Posbergh, Anna, 'Defining "Woman": A Governmentality Analysis of How
  Protective Policies Are Created in Elite Women's Sport', *International
  Review for the Sociology of Sport*, LVII/8 (2022), pp. 1350–70

Roberts, Celia, 'Tanner's Puberty Scale: Exploring the Historical
  Entanglements of Children, Scientific Photography and Sex', *Sexualities*,
  XI/3 (2016), pp. 328–46

Semenya, Caster, *The Race to Be Myself* (London, 2023)

Simpson, J. L., et al., 'Gender Verification in the Olympics', *JAMA*,
  CCLXXXIV/12 (2000), pp. 1568–9

Suits, Bernard, *The Grasshopper: Games, Life and Utopia*, 2nd edn
  (Peterborough, ON, 2005)

Tannenbaum, Cara, and Sheree Bekker, 'Sex, Gender, and Sports', *BMJ*,
  CCCLXIV (2019), i1120

Ugra, Sharda, 'World Athletics, Please Note: DSD Regulations are a Violation
  of Human Rights', *Hindustan Times*, www.hindustantimes.com,
  5 December 2020

Zhao H., et al., 'Making a "Sex-Difference Fact": Ambien Dosing at the
  Interface of Policy, Regulation, Women's Health, and Biology', *Social
  Studies of Science*, LIII/4 (2023), pp. 475–94

4 Being in Your Body

Hollick, Frederick, *The Diseases of Woman: Their Causes and Cure Familiarly
  Explained* (New York, 1847)

McCrone, Kathleen, *Playing the Game: Sport and the Physical Emancipation
  of English Women, 1870–1914* (Lexington, KY, 1988)

Manne, Kate, *Down Girl: The Logic of Misogyny* (London, 2019)

Mumford, Stephen, *A Philosopher Looks at Sport* (Cambridge, 2021)

Nussbaum, Martha, *Creating Capabilities* (Cambridge, MA, 2011)

Pavlidis, Adele, and Simone Fullagar, *Sport, Gender and Power: The Rise
  of Roller Derby* (Farnham and Burlington, VT, 2014)

Saini, Angela, *Inferior: The True Power of Women and the Science that Shows
  It* (London, 2017)

Spaaij, R., K. Farquharson and T. Marjoribanks, 'Sport and Social
  Inequalities', *Sociology Compass*, IX/5 (2015), pp. 400–411

Suits, Bernard, *The Grasshopper: Games, Life and Utopia*, 2nd edn
  (Peterborough, ON, 2005)

Sundgot-Borgen, J., et al., 'Elite Athletes Get Pregnant, Have Healthy Babies and Return to Sport Early Postpartum', *BMJ Open Sport – Exercise Medicine*, V/1 (2019)

5 Beyond the Binary

Saini, Angela, *The Patriarchs* (London, 2023)
United Nations, 'Universal Declaration of Human Rights', www.un.org, accessed 31 January 2024

6 The Future of Feminist Sport

Bishop, Cath, 'Compassion can Produce Better Performance – Just Look at the Lionesses', *The Guardian*, www.theguardian.com, 14 August 2023
Cooke, Lucy, *Bitch* (London, 2022)
Descartes, Rene, *Meditations on First Philosophy* [1641] (Cambridge, 2017)
Doyle, Jennifer, 'Capturing Semenya', https://thesportspectacle.com, 16 August 2016
Foer, Franklin, 'Megan Rapinoe Answers the Critics', *The Atlantic*, www.theatlantic.com, 22 August 2023
GenderSci Lab platform, www.genderscilab.org
Gross, Rachel E., 'Feminist Science Is Not an Oxymoron', https://undark.org, 15 September 2022
——, *Vagina Obscura: An Anatomical Voyage* (New York, 2022)
Mason, Ernest, *Womanhood in the God-Man* (London, 1891)
Stryker, Susan, and Stephen Whittle, eds, *Transgender Studies Reader* (London, 2013)
Trivers, Robert, 'Parental Investment and Sexual Selection', in *Sexual Selection and the Descent of Man, 1871–1971*, ed. B. Campbell (Chicago, IL, 1972)
Vincent, Ben, *Non-Binary Genders: Navigating Communities, Identities and Healthcare* (Bristol, 2020)

Acknowledgements

We would like to thank our many collaborators and interlocutors. In particular, we would like to thank Anna Posbergh, Simona Capisani, Sarah Teetzel and Charlene Weaving. Sheree would like to thank her collaborators in many aspects: Tracy Blake, Madeleine Pape, Holly Thorpe, Payoshni Mitra and Ryan Storr. Stephen thanks his students Imogen Hurst, Mary Atkinson and Charlotte Sellers, who produced excellent dissertations with relevance to women in sport, from which he learnt a lot. Laura Smith of Durham Roller Derby was a huge help. Chapter Three builds on material that Sheree originally published as a Twitter Note. Finally, we would like to thank all members of the Feminist Sport Lab, which we founded in 2023. We realized then that this book was not a conclusion to our work in *Feminist Sport*, but only a new beginning.

Index